Negotiating the Seed Treaty

Negotiating the Seed Treaty

Stuart Coupe and Roger Lewins

PRACTICAL ACTION
Publishing

Practical Action Publishing Ltd
25 Albert Street, Rugby, CV21 2SD, Warwickshire, UK
www.practicalactionpublishing.com

© Practical Action Publishing, 2007

First published in 2007

ISBN 10   1853396281
ISBN 13 Paperback 978 1 85339 628 1
ISBN Library Ebook: 9781780441252
Book DOI: http://dx.doi.org/10.3362/9781780441252

A catalogue record for this book is available from the British Library.

The contributors have asserted their rights under the Copyright Designs and Patents Act 1988 to be
identified as authors of their respective contributions.

Since 1974, Practical Action Publishing has published and disseminated books and information in
support of international development work throughout the world. Practical Action Publishing
(formerly ITDG Publishing) is a trading name of Intermediate Technology Publications Ltd (Company
Reg. No. 1159018), the wholly owned publishing company of Intermediate Technology Development
Group Ltd (working name Practical Action). Practical Action Publishing trades only in support of its
parent charity objectives and any profits are covenanted back to Practical Action (Charity Reg. No.
247257, Group VAT Registration No. 880 9924 76).

Cover photograph by Practical Action/Zul
Cover design by Mercer Design
Typeset by S.J.I. Services

Contents

Acknowledgements

This publication is an output of a UK Department for International Development (DFID) and Rowan Trust funded research project undertaken by Practical Action, an international NGO active on agricultural biodiversity and Farmers' Rights issues, and the Overseas Development Institute (ODI), a UK think-tank for development policy issues associated with agriculture and livelihoods. The research team comprised Stuart Coupe, Elizabeth Cromwell, John Young and Patrick Mulvany. Additional research was done by Ben Richardson and Rachel Berger.

With thanks to all the FAO officials, negotiators and researchers and civil society activists who gave the in-depth interviews and facilitated the research more generally, particularly José Esquinas Alcazar and Alvaro Toledo at the FAO Commission on Genetic Resources for Food and Agriculture, Rome.

Acronyms

AnGRFA	Animal genetic resources for food and agriculture
ASSINSEL	InternationalAssociation of Plant Breeders for the Protection of Plant Varieties
CBD	Convention on Biological Diversity
CGIAR	Consultative Group on International Agricultural Research
CGRFA	Commission on Genetic Resources for Food and Agriculture
COAG	Committee on Agriculture - a technical advisory department of FAO
CPGR	Commission on Plant Genetic Resources
CSO	Civil society organization
DFID	Department for International Development
DoC	Drivers of Change
ETC Group	Action Group on Erosion, Technology and Concentration
FAO	UN Food and Agriculture Organization
FRs	Farmers' Rights
GATT	General Agreement on Tariffs and Trade
GEF	Global Environment Facility
GM	Genetically modified
GPA	Global Plan of Action
GRAIN	Genetic Resources Action International
GURTs	Genetic Use Restriction Technologies
V-GURTs	Varieties with sterile seeds
T-GURTs	Traits triggered by environment
IARCs	International Agricultural Research Centres
IBPGR	International Bureau of Plant Genetic Resources
IMF	International Monetary Fund
IPGRI	International Plant Genetic Resources Institute
IPRs	Intellectual property rights
ITDG	Intermediate Technology Development Group (Practical Action)
IT PGRFA	International Treaty on Plant Genetic Resources for Food and Agriculture – the 'International Seed Treaty'
IU or IUPGR	International Undertaking (on Plant Genetic Resources)
MSA	Multilateral System of Access
NARCs	National Agricultural Research Centres
NGO	Non-governmental organization
ODI	Overseas Development Institute

OECD	Organization for Economic Cooperation and Development
PGRFA	Plant Genetic Resources for Food and Agriculture
PBRs	Plant breeders' rights
RAFI	Rural Advancement Foundation International (ETC Group)
RAPID	Research and Policy in Development
TRIPs	WTO Agreement on Trade Related aspects of Intellectual Property Rights
UNCTAD	United Nations Conference on Trade and Development
UNEP	United Nations Environment Programme
UNESCO	United Nations Educational Scientific and Cultural Organization
UNIDO	United Nations Industrial Development Organization
UPOV	International Union for the Protection of New Varieties of Plants
WIPO	World Intellectual Property Organization
WTO	World Trade Organization

Contributors

Murthi Anishetti, FAO, Seeds & Plant Genetic Resource Service, Rome, July 2003

Bernard le Buanec, Secretary General, International Seed Federation, Berlin, May 2004

David Cooper, CBD, June 2003 (telephone interview)

Tewolde Eghabiazer, Head of Environment Protection Agency, Ethiopia, Lead negotiator, Africa Group, London, September 2003

José (Pepe) Esquinas Alcazar, FAO, CGFRA, Rome, July 2003

Ximena Flores Palacios, IFAD, Rome, May 2004

Geoff Hawtin, former DG, IPGRI, Rome, July 2003

Toby Hodgkin, IPGRI, Rome, July 2003

Liz Hoskins, GAIA Foundation, London, September 2003

José Ramon Lopez Portillo, former Mexican Ambassador to FAO, April 2004 (telephone interview)

Arturo Martinez, FAO, Seeds & Plant Genetic Resource Service, Rome, July 2003

Francisco Martinez Gomez, former agriculture attaché of Mexico, FAO, Rome, July 2003

Pat Mooney, ETC Group, London, October 2003

Patrick Mulvany, ITDG, Rugby, March and September 2003

Andrew Mushita, Community Technology Development Trust, Harare, March 2004

Tim Roberts, Independent intellectual property specialist, Berlin, May 2004

Martin Smith, UK DEFRA/CGRFA, Rome, May 2004

Andrée Sontot, Chargée de mission, Bureau des Ressources Génétiques, Berlin, May 2004

Clive Stannard, FAO, CPRGFA, Rome, May 2004

Alvaro Toledo, FAO, CPRGFA, July 2003

Introduction

The International Seed Treaty (International Treaty on Plant Genetic Resources for Food and Agriculture—IT PGRFA) represents a major global effort to ensure the wise and fair use of crucial genetic material, today and for future generations.

The Treaty came into force on 29 June 2004, but it was the culmination of at least 20 years of negotiations involving a diverse array of interests that together developed a greater public awareness of the threat of genetic erosion and of the central role of role of farmers as custodians of these resources. The Treaty was a significant achievement in that it cross-cut the interests of many existing agencies and international commitments with related but sometimes contradictory roles.

This paper examines the process by which the main arguments emerged and how key players in the process worked to influence the negotiation and eventual adoption of the Treaty. Five key periods or 'transition episodes' are identified and outlined in detail.

Central to the Treaty is the attempt to establish a multilateral system of access to plant genetic resources for food and agriculture based on an accepted list of key plant varieties and an acknowledged mechanism for benefit sharing. In parallel, the Treaty aims to recognize and protect Farmers' Rights—the rights of farmers to access and use this material and to be rewarded and respected as managers and custodians of these resources. It is also the international legal instrument for implementing the 1996 Leipzig Global Plan of Action. These issues are explored in detail.

The evolution of the Treaty is then analysed with respect to the role of research, individuals and coalitions and changes in the political landscape. The civil society and non-governmental organizations that represented the interests of the South were well-organized and developed strategies to influence the policy discourse at an early stage. These groups drew on the expertise and influence of key individuals with a scientific background and reputation within agricultural research to ensure that the debate encompassed issues relating to rights, equity and other aspects of genetic diversity.

Finally, the significance of the Treaty is discussed in relation to the continued threat to plant genetic resources for food and agriculture, dangerous trends in ownership and breeder technology and threats to other agricultural heritage, in particular the alarming loss of animal breeds.

1

The need for the International Seed Treaty

The agriculture that is practised around the world today is the product of at least 12,000 years of selection, adaptation and innovation by farmers. Plants and animals have been selected by humans to provide food and other products on the basis of productivity, disease resistance and nutritional value, among other traits. A number of species have evolved with humans, who have selected and developed a huge number of varieties of these species, each with particular characteristics that fit with the local landscape and micro-environment and the needs of communities. This legacy of agricultural biodiversity is immense and ensures that agriculture can adapt to local and global shocks and trends like new pests and diseases and climate change. This diversity ensures that millions of people can practise agriculture well-suited to the local environmental setting and the needs of communities. In short, genetic diversity is an asset globally, but one that is especially important for the poor who are reliant on natural resources for their livelihoods.

However, this heritage is derived from a remarkably small number of original species, and the world's population is now reliant on a diminishing number of varieties and major crops. Of the 7,000 edible plant species, about 120 are used frequently, only 12 or so cultivated species provide 90% of the world's food, and of these only four (rice, wheat, maize and potatoes) account for more than 50% of dietary energy globally.

Global food security, now and for future generations, can draw only from this pool of diversity. The rate of decline in this diversity is alarming and is increasing. It is estimated that some 90-95% of farmers' varieties have been lost in the last century and that the rate of loss is now about 2% per year. In the case of animal breeds the loss is even greater, with about one breed being lost each month.

What is causing this loss, and on such a scale? Modern systems of ownership, in conjunction with new breeding technologies and the ability to separate different components of plant genotypes, have meant that large companies have the ability to sell modified forms and displace the use of traditional varieties. Commercial innovation and restrictive patents directly and indirectly challenge the rights of around 1.6 billion farmers who depend on farm-saved seed and other important systems such as local seed trade and exchange. The commercial system of collection, modification and variety protection can equate to biopiracy, whereby genetic heritage is commandeered by powerful interests at the expense of users. In addition, new technical developments such as Genetic Use Restriction Technologies (GURTs or terminator technologies) will further threaten the capacity of farmers to manage their own crops and seed for local needs. The realization that the genetic basis of crops has been eroding has stimulated interest in the local and indigenous systems of knowledge that enable the ongoing management and *in situ* conservation of varieties associated with food and agriculture. However, many of these practices, such as on-farm seed saving and sharing, appear incompatible with formal patent systems and the agencies that exist to regulate intellectual property rights (IPRs).

It is now internationally acknowledged that this agricultural heritage must be preserved and protected both *ex situ* in seed banks and public and private collections and, crucially, *in situ* in farmers' fields, where these varieties undergo continuous modification, selection and adaptation to the changing environment.

The core international response to this threat has been the development of the International Seed Treaty (International Treaty on Plant Genetic Resources for Food and Agriculture—IT PGRFA), a concerted effort to lay out global ground rules for access to and use of PGRFA. The Treaty is a major achievement that links agriculture, trade and the environment and affects the interests and responsibilities of a vast range of stakeholders.

The IT PGRFA aims to promote the conservation and sustainable use of the genetic resources of all the world's food crops, implement a multilateral system of access to a list of some of the world's most essential food and fodder crops, and ensure that benefits from the commercial use of the genetic resources of these crops are returned to farmers in developing countries (FAO, 2002). The Treaty was agreed in November 2001 under the auspices of the UN Food and Agriculture Organization (FAO) and entered into force on 29 June 2004.

The Treaty covers all plant genetic resources of importance to agriculture, but for some 64 key food crops and 29 forage species it establishes a unique *Multilateral System of Access and Benefit Sharing*. Benefits are to be shared through information exchange, technology transfer, capacity building, and the mandatory sharing of the profits of commercialization.

It has a clause that prohibits, with some qualification, patents that restrict access to seeds. It thereby provides an alternate model for the governance of the intellectual property associated with plant genetic resources for food and agriculture to the World Trade Organization's Agreement on Trade Related aspects of Intellectual Property Rights (TRIPs) Article 27.3(b).[1]

A crucial component within the Treaty relates to Farmers' Rights and makes provision for the protection of traditional knowledge and the participation of farmers in management and the sharing of benefits.

The debate over access and management of PGRFA can be caricatured as one represented by the interests of the plant breeding industry on the one hand and farmers' interests and their CSO and NGO advocates on the other. The plant breeders are increasingly dominated by global biotechnology corporations and are dependent on the thousands of varieties developed by farmers over generations, continuously returning to these fields in search of new strains. In turn, there is a well-organized movement defending the importance and legitimacy of indigenous seed systems and the rights of farmers, both in the North and the South. As the true custodians of plant and animal genetic resources, it is argued, small-scale farmers should be recognized as legitimate and principal partners in their management and use, with formal access rights to material and to the benefits derived through research and development. In the 1990s, new thinking on the vital role of 'landraces' was consolidated into an 'ecosystem approach' to agriculture, emphasizing the sustainability and ecological services provided by small scale farming around the world.

A complex network of groups with overlapping interests has developed to represent the concerns of the South and to fight for policy changes in support of small-scale farmers. For instance, the grassroots constituency has lobbied governments and the FAO directly and has approached the FAO Commission on Plant Genetic Resources through established Farmers' movements such as Via Campesina. In parallel, Northern and Southern NGOs and individuals have played a key role in publicizing the various threats posed by the growing monopolization of genetic resources and the erosion of diversity.

Many meetings, statements, and events over two decades contributed to the crystallization of a certain set of views shared by civil society actors, government negotiators, scientists and researchers, which laid the basis for agreement. The discussions accommodated a broad range of concerns and established a much deeper understanding of the issues across a wide audience.

The next chapter discusses in detail how the Treaty evolved from a series of informal discussions and formal meetings and the role played by key individuals and interest groups.

Note

1 'Members may also exclude from patentability: plants and animals other than micro-organisms, and essentially biological processes for the production of plants and animals other than non-biological and micro-biological processes. However, members shall provide for the protection of plant varieties either by patent or by an effective *sui generis* system.'

2

The history of the International Seed Treaty

Ownership of, and access to, genetic resources in food and agriculture were first recognized as issues requiring regulation in work conducted in the early 1970s by a small and committed cadre of agronomists concerned with declining global plant genetic diversity. The gravity of the issue was somewhat obscured by the crop yield increases achieved in the Green Revolution and an extended period of increasing uptake of high-response crop varieties in developing country agriculture. In such a setting, there was limited global interest in the negative and longer-term impacts on plant genetic resources. The fair and sustainable management of this diversity was something of a fringe issue.

Knowledge gaps and a lack of awareness represented a huge barrier to promoting the issue of genetic erosion to policy stakeholders. Governments in both the North and South were generally poorly informed and unaware of the importance of maintaining stocks of plant genetic diversity for future food and agriculture needs. This genetic heritage was overlooked by Southern governments, in part, because neither the issue nor the genetic resources could apparently meet short-term political objectives or national development goals. In essence there was a *'profound disconnect between the value of agricultural biodiversity and the North's willingness to pay'* (RAFI, 2001).

However, trends in genetic erosion and a real threat of accelerated loss and restricted access inspired several key NGOs and individuals already involved in rural development advocacy. It was not until the late 1970s and early 1980s that evidence of inequalities over ownership of and access to plant genetic resources was presented in a manner linking the huge potential economic benefits for industrial interests with the resultant skewed power over global food security. This is what caught the attention of leading Southern diplomats in the UN Food and Agriculture Organization.

This new movement argued that if the genetic base of the major food crops narrowed, and there was no recourse to farmers' knowledge, these crops could become highly vulnerable to plant pests and diseases. Although *ex situ* collections of plant varieties in gene banks existed, this material was not exposed to environmental change or the gradual refinement and selection by farmers over generations. *Ex situ* material is a crucial resource but, it was argued, the management and control of this resource must be carefully regulated to prevent monopolization of access and benefits, and the resource must be managed in conjunction with a system that allows farmers to continue using, saving and developing their own varieties.

The issue of gene banks and their regulation became one associated with North-South equity and justice. Through the 1960s and 1970s, the International Agricultural Research Centres (IARCs) and National Agricultural Research Centres (NARCs) accumulated the main collections of germ-plasm, mostly held in Northern industrialized countries. (see Box 1).

Suspicions and distrust began to emerge in the early 1980s over ownership of this genetic material and the right to determine its use. A vigorous new discourse was developed by NGOs on the injustices of the situation: that the North had

> **Box 1. The role of the IARCs and NARCs**
>
> The International Agricultural Research Centres (IARCs) and National Agricultural Research Centres (NARCs) have a key role in the conservation of the world's PGRFA and the significance of their role is likely to increase with the implementation of the Treaty. The IARCs are especially important and hold approximately 10% of the six million accessions in *ex situ* collections but the quality and coverage of these collections makes them especially significant. Globally, a large but unknown number of the total accessions in storage are thought to be duplicates and the number of 'unique' samples may be a third or less of the total. The CG Centres hold over half a million seed samples in *ex situ* storage, representing some 40% of all unique samples held by genebanks worldwide. These seeds have been collected from all regions of the globe and from farmers in the developing world. The CGIAR collections are generally better catalogued than National collections and the collections contain a large proportion of key 'landraces', highly diverse 'farmers' varieties'. Approximately 59% of the CGIAR materials are landraces, compared with only 12%, on average, for government genebanks, and 3% for private genebanks (Pistorious, 1995).
>
> The CGIAR collections were assembled during a time when Plant Genetic Resources for Agriculture (PGRFA) were considered 'the common heritage of humankind'. There was an implicit, and sometimes explicit, guarantee that the collections would remain in the 'public domain', cared for by the CGIAR, but available for all to use. However, the legal status of the material within the IARC genebanks was unclear.

stolen the genetic resources of the South and allowed them to be used to advance the interests of agribusiness corporations. The research community and industry at the heart of the Green Revolution were offended by this attack on what they saw as a crucial contribution to food production and development, for example in South and South-east Asia.

At this stage, the International Bureau of Plant Genetic Resources (IBPGR), in Rome, was responsible for co-ordinating a loose global network of gene banks. Technically an NGO, the IBPGR was a quasi UN organization that functioned 'as an overseer of northern interests' (Mooney, 1988, 285). It opposed all developing-country initiatives at FAO, 'under a technical and scientific veneer', with its senior staff becoming highly involved in undermining the proposal for a new global public gene bank under UN control.

From these unpromising beginnings, the FAO has steered countless meetings, statements and events over two decades, involving a long, fraught and increasingly expansive intergovernmental policy process. This process culminated in the adoption of the International Treaty on Plant Genetic Resources for Food and Agriculture on 3 November 2001 and, after its ratification in April 2004 by 78 countries, its entry into force on 29 June 2004.

The development of the Treaty is a major breakthrough in an area of international policy that for 20 years had been highly contested by the interests and representatives of agriculture, trade, intellectual property rights, rural development and the environment (Figure 1).

The following agencies are major formal stakeholders in PGRFA and its use and management, conservation and trade.

FAO

Since its foundation in 1945, the Food and Agriculture Organization of the United Nations has been intended to be a neutral forum in the global effort to identify policies and activities that promote production and sustainability in agriculture, fisheries and forests. Many of its activities are research and knowledge based, and

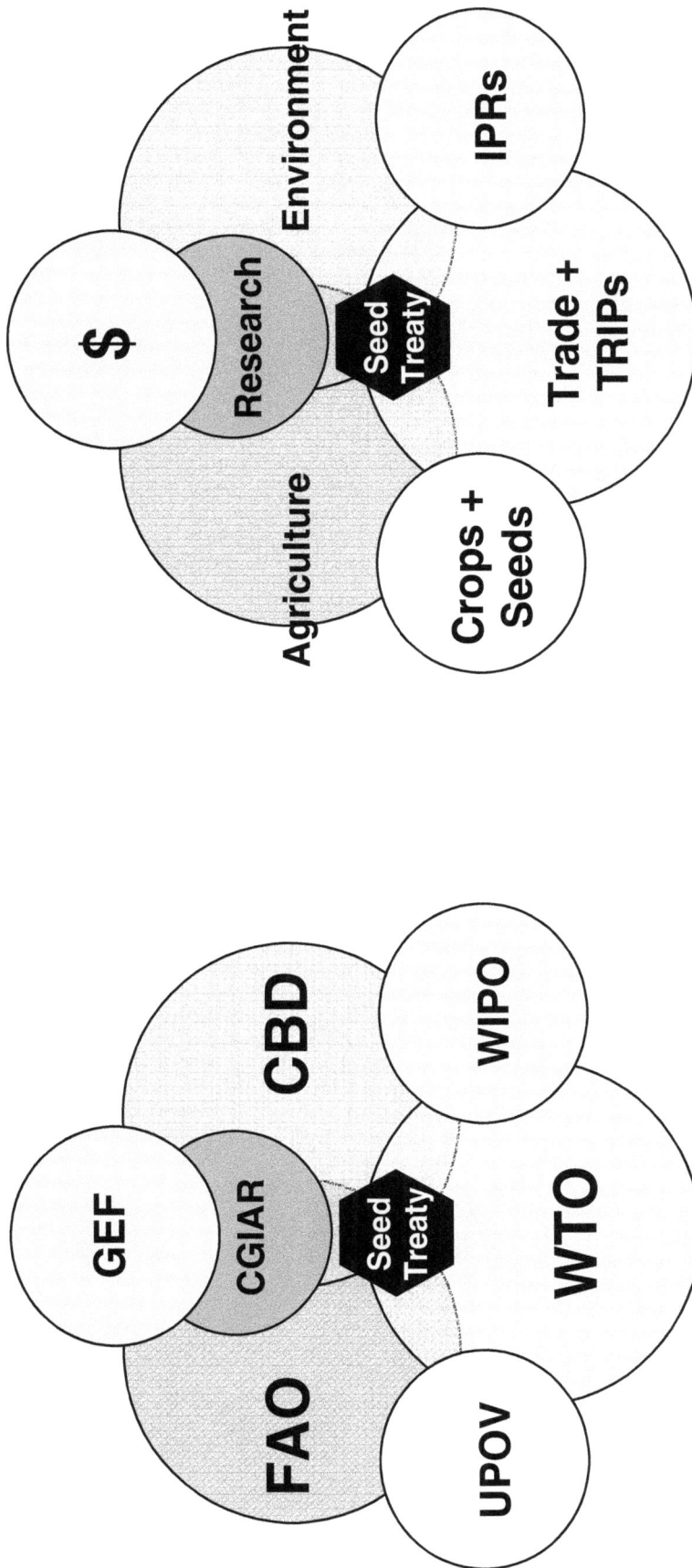

Figure 1. The key agencies and their relationship to the management of PGRFA. The International Seed Treaty is as at the crossroads between agriculture, trade and the environment (thanks to Patrick Mulvany).

there is great emphasis on the dissemination of information for modernization, disease and pest control and increased efficiency. The FAO's mandate is *'to raise levels of nutrition, improve agricultural productivity, better the lives of rural populations and contribute to the growth of the world economy'*.

CBD

The Convention on Biological Diversity was signed by 150 countries in 1992 and was intended *inter alia* to help implement Agenda 21. The CBD extends beyond *ex situ* conservation and acknowledges the social and economic role of biodiversity and related trade. 'The importance of the biodiversity challenge was universally acknowledged at the United Nations Conference on Environment and Development, which met in Rio de Janeiro in 1992, and through the development of the Convention on Biological Diversity. In ratifying the Convention, the Parties have committed themselves to undertaking national and international measures aimed at its achieving three objectives: the conservation of biological diversity; the sustainable use of its components; and the fair and equitable sharing of benefits arising out of the utilization of genetic resources.'

CGIAR

The Consultative Group on International Agricultural Research was created in 1971 as an alliance of national governments, international and regional organizations, and private foundations supporting 15 International Agricultural Centres to work with national agricultural research systems, civil society and the private sector. CGIAR aims to reduce poverty, foster human well-being, promote agricultural growth and protect the environment through science. CGIAR operates in over 100 countries and covers agroforestry, biodiversity, food, forage and tree crops, pro-environment farming techniques, fisheries, forestry, livestock, food policies and agricultural research services. Thirteen of the Centres are based in developing countries.

WTO

The World Trade Organization, established in 1995, is a negotiation forum for trade. Its remit is largely based on the 1986–94 Uruguay Round and the General Agreement on Tariffs and Trade (GATT). Therefore, trade liberalization is its central objective, but WTO extends beyond the coverage of GATT to include services and IPRs.

UPOV

The International Union for the Protection of New Varieties of Plants was established by the International Convention for the Protection of New Varieties of Plants and came into force in 1968; substantial revisions took place in 1978 and 1991. Countries or intergovernmental organizations wishing to join UPOV must have laws on plant variety protection in line with the Convention. There are 55 member countries, of which 44 subscribe to UPOV 91. While UPOV 78 is still valid, UPOV 91 is a much tougher version. It better suits a breeding world divided between conventional breeders and biotechnologists. In essence, the 1991 revision brought Plant Breeders Rights closer to patents. The most important change in UPOV 91 was the virtual elimination of both the farmers' privilege and breeders' exemption. Member countries that sign the 91 rules 'may' permit farmers to keep seeds and other propagation material from protected varieties for use on their own farms, but it will no longer be an automatic right. At the same time, breeders face new restrictions on the free use of genetic material, since the holder of a variety may now limit the right of another breeder to develop, produce, sell, stock or simply use any variety which is 'essentially derived' from a previously protected variety. UPOV's mission is 'to provide and promote an effective system of plant variety protection, with the aim of encouraging the development of new varieties of plants, for the benefit of society'. It has been argued that the property rights (sui generis) system adopted by UPOV supports the interests of plant breeders in the North and could threaten agricultural biodiversity. UPOV promotes itself as the *sui generis* option for TRIPS 27.3(b).

WIPO

The World Intellectual Property Organization is an agency of the United Nations dedicated to establishing an international intellectual property rights (IPRs) system. It was established by the WIPO Convention in 1967 with a mandate to promote IPRs globally. WIPO's objective of a consistent and globally recognized IPR system is controversial with respect to PGRFA because, whilst facilitating transnational control, it could undermine the capacity of developing countries to protect and manage their PGRFA heritage for national objectives.

GEF

The Global Environment Facility, established in 1991, provides financial backing to projects and programmes in the developing world that aim to support the environment. *'GEF is an independent financial organization that provides grants to developing countries for projects that benefit the global environment and promote sustainable livelihoods in local communities.'* Operational Programme 13 is for agricultural biodiversity.

There are three principal interacting institutions that needed to be influenced for coherent policy to emerge:

- The FAO Commission on GRFA, responsible for the IT PGRFA negotiations,
- The Conference of the Parties to the CBD, and
- The Consultative Group for International Agricultural Research, due to its role in the protection of *ex situ* collections of PGRFA in its gene banks.

This paper represents an overview of the key stages in the development of the Treaty and its significance for future management of PGRFA. Five 'transition episodes' are identified that were particularly important in shaping the direction of the negotiations and maintaining momentum towards the objective of an international agreement. In each of the episodes selected, the PGRFA policy process was affected by changes in the global political and institutional context to which its protagonists had to adapt and develop new positions and strategies.[1]

2.1 Formation of the Commission on Plant Genetic Resources and the International Undertaking (1983)

In the 1970s and early 1980s, the issue of ownership and regulation of plant genetic resources had crystallized into a sharp North-South political divide. The great significance and controversy surrounding the issue prompted the FAO in 1983 to adopt the International Undertaking on Plant Genetic Resources (IU). The Commission set up to manage the IU was unusual in that its establishment was not by consensus, but came about as the result of a contested vote at the 1983 FAO Conference. Its creation was vigorously opposed by the scientific establishment based at the International Bureau on Plant Genetic Resources (IBPGR) and by the industrialized countries.

One of the first FAO representatives to publicly acknowledge the concerns of the South and to call for some form of international gene bank under UN control was the Spaniard José (Pepe) Esquinas-Alcazar. His progressive political convictions were rare amongst the technical staff at Rome, and his pronouncements contrasted with those of most other FAO functionaries of the time. He was soon discouraged from having any formal meetings with FAO delegates from developing countries (Equinas, Interview).

At this stage, Southern representatives to the IBPGR were elected by technical departments and institutions with little accompanying interest or input from governmental level. The capacity of these representatives to contribute to the process and influence proceedings was limited as a result. Francisco Martinez Gomez (2002), a member of the Mexican delegation to the FAO, describes how the majority of Southern representatives were timid and poorly briefed in comparison to their Northern colleagues and how this patron-client relationship reflected the disparity in scientific and technical resources of the time. The NGOs recognized this gap in the democratic process and started mobilizing interest in the issues with and on behalf of Southern interests. Esquinas was able to work informally with the NGOs, who would in turn engage the Southern delegates.

Other individuals also played a major role in highlighting and legitimizing these concerns within and outside the FAO. As a key architect of the Green Revolution and respected plant scientist, Professor M.S. Swaminathan made the first official reference to North-South issues of gene flow at the FAO in his capacity as Independent Chairman of the FAO Council. Swaminathan had been influenced by *Seeds of the Earth*, prepared by Pat Mooney of the Canadian NGO Rural Advancement Foundation International (RAFI) for the UN Conference on Science, Technology and Development, Vienna, August 1979.

The 1979 FAO Conference, chaired by Spain, was significant because Esquinas had gained some support for a proposal for an international gene bank under the auspices of the UN. The idea was then developed by the International Consumers' Union NGO coalition and championed at the FAO in 1981, where Pat Mooney and the NGOs called for a global gene bank, a $300m fund for a genetic resources convention and the establishment of an FAO Commission specialized in PGRFA.

Despite this, the seed companies and biotech corporations were content with the *status quo* and worked to persuade governments and UN organizations not to take any action on the Mexican demands. As a result, initially sympathetic European governments withdrew their support from the small group of developing country delegates in Rome despite the efforts of Mexican delegates to counteract this and attempt to persuade a core group of supportive diplomats.

The early 1980s represented a new world order that appeared to exacerbate differences in North-South politics and interests, but this was being countered by strategic coalitions and diplomatic solidarities among Southern states. Mexico's initiative at the FAO attracted support from leading Latin American countries. Under the leadership of Mexico and a handful of FAO insiders and NGO activists, this new group began to lobby for assurances that Cold War politics would not impinge on the exchange of germ-plasm and that the South would not be denied access to genetic material originating from their own countries but now stored in the North.

The role of informal face-to-face dialogue between certain leading players was crucial at this early stage in the negations on PGRFA. For instance, the FAO Director General, Edouard Saouma of Lebanon, was closely associated with several Southern diplomats and gave his personal support to a Mexican proposal to investigate the possibility of establishing a Commission. Under pressure from Northern delegates, however, this proposal was referred to the Committee on Agriculture (COAG), a technical advisory department within the FAO, with the intention of blocking it. At the corresponding COAG meeting in November 1981, Pat Mooney, as the sole NGO representative, presented a dramatic report drawing on IBPGR data and demonstrating an overwhelming net donation of genetic resources from Southern states to the North.

This provided the basis for two days of speeches on what had initially been scheduled a one-hour agenda item. Intransigent US and Swedish attitudes helped maintain the dialogue by provoking the indignation of the Southern diplomats.

In 1983, the G77 (see Box 2) formed a contact group to help the General Secretary of the FAO re-launch the gene bank proposal at COAG (Martinez, 2002, 113). Under the leadership of Mexico, the G77 managed to force a resolution committing the FAO to a feasibility study on a global gene bank. Later that year, the Minister of Agriculture of the newly elected government of Spain offered to host the gene bank. This move was highly significant because it effectively challenged the Northern consensus to block the proposal.

The COAG feasibility study was presented later in 1983, but was immediately countered by representations from Genetic Resources Action International (GRAIN) and RAFI, highlighting injustices in the proposed location and the control of genetic resources. The growing tension and increasing stakes attracted the world's media and expanded global coverage and public awareness of the issue.

To coincide with the November 1983 FAO Conference, the Dag Hammarskjold Foundation published 'The Law of the Seed' by Pat Mooney as a special issue of its journal, *Development Dialogue*. Hundreds of copies were brought to Rome, and the impact on the delegates was dramatic. The resulting furore helped raise the issue of fair and regulated access and forced serious consideration of the Mexican-led proposal for new formal FAO structures with responsibility for the governance of genetic resources.

Box 2. The Group of 77

The Group of 77 (G-77) was established on 15 June 1964 by 77 developing country signatories of the 'Joint Declaration of the Seventy-Seven Countries' issued at the end of the first session of the United Nations Conference on Trade and Development (UNCTAD) in Geneva. Beginning with the first Ministerial Meeting of the Group of 77 in Algiers in 1967, a permanent institutional structure gradually developed which led to the creation of Chapters of the Group of 77 in Rome (FAO), Vienna (UNIDO), Paris (UNESCO), Nairobi (UNEP) and the Group of 24 in Washington DC (IMF and World Bank). Although the membership of the G-77 has since increased to 133 countries, the original name has been retained because of its historic significance.

As the largest coalition in the United Nations, G-77 provides a basis for the developing world to articulate and promote its collective economic interests and enhance its joint negotiating capacity on all major international economic issues in the United Nations system. G-77 also aims to promote economic and technical cooperation among the developing countries, themselves.

The result was the International Undertaking (IU), a voluntary international agreement explicitly aiming to harmonize access to PGRFA (Box 3). Further hard bargaining ensured the Mexican delegation was successful in its demands for a new and permanent Commission within the FAO.

The new discourse was sufficiently strong and coherent to bring major institutional innovations at the FAO, i.e. the establishment of a new responsible UN policy body Commission on Plant Genetic Resources (CPGR) and the IU, with a clause challenging the prevailing orthodoxies on intellectual property rights on PGRFA.

Powerful interests like the biotechnology industry may disregard United Nations initiatives if their impact is of marginal political significance. The period of 1981–83, however, ensured that the issue of germ-plasm and seed was firmly on the map as a policy issue, both for the G-77 and globally. A total North-South impasse would have had very serious consequences for Northern scientists and breeders by limiting their access to plant genetic material.

The period 1989–91 demonstrates how the serious North-South rift of the 1980s had been overcome, making way for meaningful negotiations and consensus, including the agreement on additional clauses in the IU, such as resolution 5/89 on Farmers' Rights. In the mid 1980s the IU, its remit, and its significance, were still open to interpretation. It was broadly agreed that genetic resources are the common heritage of humankind and should be accessible to all. The problem lay in the definition of 'genetic resources'. Northern interests questioned the inclusion of commercialized varieties, and opponents of the IU were already able to point to what they saw as contradictions with other processes where plant breeders were entitled to restrict access to 'material under development'. In addition, there was a very real danger that the IU was at odds with another powerful institution, the International Union for the Protection of New Varieties of Plants (UPOV).

Despite the efforts of the US, which had lobbied to block change, by 1987 more than 100 countries had signed up as members of the CPGR. The 1987 session of the CPGR focused on discussion of a series of reports commissioned to clarify key issues. These reports included studies of the legal status of collections, including seed legislation and plant breeders' rights, with a view to the potential establishment of an international network of germ-plasm banks under the jurisdiction of the FAO. Other important reports were presented on the status of *in situ* conservation of plant genetic resources and the feasibility of establishing an international

---

Box 3. Key clauses in and membership of the 1983 International Undertaking.

Plant Genetic Resources are a heritage of mankind and should consequently be available without restriction.
Plant Genetic Resources: a reproductive or vegetative propagating material of the following categories of plants;
    i)   Cultivated varieties
    ii)   Obsolete cultivars
    iii) Primitive cultivars (land races)
    iv) Wild and weed species, near relatives of cultivated varieties
    v)   Special genetic stock (including elite and current breeders' lines and mutants).
One hundred and thirteen countries have adhered to the Undertaking, which seeks to 'ensure that plant genetic resources of economic and/or social interest, particularly for agriculture, will be explored, preserved, evaluated and made available for plant breeding and scientific purposes'. It is monitored by the Commission on Plant Genetic Resources (CPGR) [Later to become the CGRFA for Food and Agriculture (CGRFA)].
Source: http://www.fao.org/ag/cgrfa/IU.htm

fund for plant genetic resources. These reports worked well in clarifying the under-lying issues of genetic conservation and helped remove the polarization of posi-tions that was a legacy of previous meetings. This helped ensure that the FAO Con-ference Resolution 5 of 1989 acknowledged the coexistence of Plant Breeders' Rights and Farmers' Rights (see Chapter 4 for a discussion of the role of evidence in the formulation of the Seed Treaty).

In summary, this period represents a crucial stage in the formulation of the Treaty and related structures. Before 1983 there were neither the processes nor the struc-tures for decision-making about the conservation and use of PGRFA. Financial support from donor countries targeted scientific research at the IBPGR, the aims and scope of which were not accountable to Southern governments. According to Martinez Gomez (2002), the IU is a testament to the fact that it is possible in a complex multilateral forum, such as FAO, for various discordant networks and in-terests to converge around an alternative discourse which counteracts the drive towards the commercialization of knowledge and genetic resources.

Despite this progress, firm political commitment to sustainable and equitable access for Southern interests and farmers was still lacking. As the debate contin-ued, the media in Europe and North America finally took notice. Plant breeder corporations pushed for intellectual property legislation but found themselves fiercely opposed by farmers, churches and advocacy groups. Very real differences in priorities and approach were exacerbated by sensational media reports and by the lack of direct communication between adversaries. The controversy placed the topic of genetic resources in the public realm, increasing awareness and attracting addi-tional support for conservation programmes and Farmers' Rights. However, this new politicization threatened to damage plant breeders' interests, possibly imped-ing the exchange of genetic resources and harming breeding and conservation programmes. While some individuals within plant breeding corporations, govern-ments and NGOs maintained a hard line approach to the debate, others began to see the need for a conciliatory effort. The 'Keystone dialogues' were born out of this concern.

2.2 The Keystone Dialogues (1989–91)

In addition to the formal sessions in Rome, this period featured the Keystone Dia-logues, a set of informal meetings running from 1989 to 1991 that served to build understanding between the chief protagonists. On the one hand, Northern gov-ernments and scientists had to move beyond their earlier intransigence, while on the other, Southern governments and Civil Society Organizations had to develop a more dispassionate and evidence-based rhetoric (Mooney, 1998).

In 1988, the Keystone Center in Colorado agreed to act as a 'neutral facilitator' in an international dialogue on plant genetic resources. The first plenary meeting focused on *ex situ* conservation, with subsequent plenary meetings convened in Chennai, India, and Norway. Working group and steering committee meetings were held in Leningrad, Ottawa, Rome and Uppsala, and worked to bring together many of the prominent individuals involved in genetic conservation, including the heads of the US, Soviet Union, Chinese, Indian, Brazilian, Ethiopian, Nordic and Dutch genetic resources programs. Well-known corporate officials from North America, South America and Europe attended and government, FAO, World Bank, and Con-sultative Group on International Agricultural Research (CGIAR) officials were in-volved. Grassroots farm organizations, advocacy groups and distinguished inde-pendent scientists were also represented. According to Cary Fowler (1993), '*The informal and off-the-record style of the meetings helped dissolve many encrusted views and personal antagonisms which had built up over the years. The trust and, indeed, friendships which grew out of the meetings facilitated some rather remarkable policy breakthroughs'.*

The Keystone Dialogue participants endorsed the establishment of a Fund that would recognize "Farmers' Rights" and that would support genetic resources conservation and utilization. The Fund was intended to identify and compensate individuals, but also to acknowledge farmers as a special group and assist them in conservation and sustainable management. This idea was immediately adopted by the FAO Conference in 1991 and annexed to the IU in resolution 3/91.

By 1991, the Dialogues had yielded the following breakthroughs:

- A new consultative atmosphere with international recognition of the need for the protection of germ-plasm was achieved.
- There was a demand for US$300m to operate the policy process.
- Grassroots innovators and their representatives were included and established their voice; the notion that farmers had a unique role in the conservation and management of germ-plasm became well established.
- The recommendation of a formal role for advocacy and civil society organizations was made.
- There was an acknowledgement of the limitations of a conventional intellectual property rights approach to PGRFA and a need for a debate on alternatives within the FAO.
- The right of farmers to save seeds was acknowledged, as was the right of breeders to exclude their modified lines from open exchange.
- It was agreed that Southern countries should be granted the right to withhold material of potential commercial value.

However, despite these improved relations between parties, the discussions at the FAO remained deadlocked over financing. Donor countries would not make money available without concessions on germ-plasm access, which the South was not prepared to make. A real threat to any new consensus was posed by United States initiatives at the General Agreement on Tariffs and Trade (GATT) that attempted to force developing countries to adopt and recognize Western-style intellectual property laws for biological materials. These laws do not recognize the creative contributions of the 'informal' (farmer-community) sector, and effectively exclude such farmers from benefiting from the resources they have identified, developed, and nurtured for years. In Europe and North America, attempts to circumscribe or eliminate the right of farmers to save seed of protected cultivars would generate further controversy.[2]

Box 4. The Global Plan of Action

The adoption of the GPA in 1996 was significant because it represented the first international and concerted effort to outline a path to coordinated use and conservation of PGRFA in the face of increasing industry ownership and control. The GPA acknowledged serious shortcomings with the PGRFA collections and the bias towards *ex situ* conservation over sustainability at the farm level and outlines prospects for restoring traditional seed supplies and supporting wild foods for indigenous communities.

The GPA outlines 20 priority activities for the conservation and management of PGRFA though *ex situ* and *in situ* strategies, the use of PGRFA and the required institutional structures. It was subsequently recognised by the CBD and ultimately formed a central part of the IT PGRFA.

Critics of the GPA highlight its focus on technical and *ex situ* strategies via the CGIAR that serve the plant breeding industry rather than farmers' interests and the absence of a strategy to deal with trade, the WTO and IPRs (see GRAIN, May 1996).

These issues continued to dominate negotiations in the years that followed, but the Keystone Dialogues represented a significant milestone in the evolution of the International Seed Treaty. In particular, the Dialogues helped set the agenda and scope of the Global Plan of Action adopted by 150 countries at the Leipzig International Technical Conference in 1996 (Box 4).

2.3 The Nairobi Final Act (1992)

Preparations at UNEP for the 1992 Rio Earth Summit and the Convention on Biological Diversity were moving the debate on the management of genetic resources in a different direction. The notion of common heritage was giving way to national sovereignty and country-level administration, with a new onus on the state to govern genetic heritage or to recognize the special rights of distinct groups.

In 1991, the CPGR passed a resolution recognizing the sovereign rights of nations over their genetic resources and agreed that Farmers' Rights should be implemented through a new international fund. The IU, with its bold statement on common heritage that now featured an annex asserting national sovereignty, was weakened by contradictions.

The notion of genetic resources as a common heritage of mankind received a hammer blow at the Preparatory Committee for the CBD in Geneva when the G77 turned its back on common heritage in favour of the prospect of sharing benefits from biotechnology.

The text of the CBD was agreed on 12 May 1992 at Nairobi in what is known as the Nairobi Final Act. The focus was overwhelmingly on non-agricultural biodiversity, with fewer than 10% of delegates at the meeting associated with agriculture. Recognizing this serious weakness, David Cooper and others, notably Pat Mooney helped secure Resolution 3, 'Interrelationship between the CBD and the promotion of sustainable agriculture', a statement acknowledging the special case of agricultural biodiversity and calling on the FAO to reshape the IU in harmony with the CBD. This gave the IU a new lease of life and established a clearer mandate for negations post-Rio.

Resolution 3 was the result of last minute and desperate negotiations, without which the IU would probably have been relegated to being a minor instrument with little capacity to renegotiate its role in relation to CBD. It would have taken years of lobbying within CBD to rectify the situation, to promote the IU within the UN system and to develop an effective governance structure for GRFA.

2.4 The FAO-CGIAR accord (1993–94)

From the beginning of the FAO negotiations post-Rio, the National and International Centres and the genetic resource collections of the Consultative Group on International Agricultural Research were a major focus for delegates. In 1993, Jose Esquinas proposed that the CGRFA should embark upon a major revision of the IU and make it a legally binding convention in harmony with the CBD. At this stage, civil society organizations were concerned that the informality of the Keystone Dialogues would be lost and that a more legalistic process would result in compromise or total failure (Mooney 1994).

At a heated closing of the Second Session of the Intergovernmental Committee on the Convention on Biological Diversity, held June–July 1994 in Nairobi, 112 governments unanimously called for the establishment of intergovernmental control over the genetic resources held in the gene banks of the IARCs. The meeting specifically called on the FAO to reach agreement with the CG Centres to grant the IARCs trusteeship over the germ-plasm as soon as possible. This decision was tabled by the Intergovernmental Committee with the specific aim of halting a World Bank initiative to seize control of the seed stocks that form the basis of world agriculture.

Although the CBD had set out to establish new systems of equity in access to the world's genetic resources, the *ex situ* collections had been omitted from planning. Efforts to establish intergovernmental authority over the CGIAR's international collections were threatened in the mid 1990s by what many thought was the sudden intention of the World Bank to scuttle any agreement with the FAO and the CBD on access, ownership and the sharing of benefits associated with these materials.

The World Bank's supposed strategy was brought to the attention of the governments in Nairobi by about 40 major environmental and development NGOs after they had received a letter from the Vice President of the Bank and current Chair of the CGIAR saying that *'it would be foolhardy to lock* [the international collections held by the IARCs] *into* [such] *agreements'*. This strategy came at the very moment that the individual IARCs were on the verge of signing the accord on trusteeship and intergovernmental authority for the collections with the FAO.

The NGO response was immediate, presenting the World Bank stance as a 'coup attempt' and 'dawn raid' on the world's genetic heritage to the global media. At the end of the 1994 intergovernmental meeting in Nairobi, over 30 countries took the floor to express their concern on this matter, which had dominated the two week session. According to the report of the meeting, governments *'strongly supported the efforts to bring* [the CGIAR's germ-plasm collections] *under the auspices of FAO'*. Specifically, *'Delegates expressed strong support for finalizing the agreement between the FAO and the IARCs as soon as possible'*.

Geoffrey Hawtin, as the Director of the International Plant Genetic Resources Institute (IPGRI – see Box 5), speaking formally on behalf of the CGIAR, rejected the World Bank position and repeated the international demand for the CGIAR collections to be granted the legal and political status required for intergovernmental management.

The role of NGOs such as RAFI and Genetic Resources Action International (GRAIN) in lobbying governments in Nairobi and forcing this climb down should not be underestimated.

Box 5. The structure and remit of the International Plant Genetic Resources Institute (CGIAR, 2004).

IPGRI was established as a legal entity under international law in October 1991 and recognized as such by the host country, Italy, through parliamentary ratification in January 1994. Its operations started in 1994, evolving from the International Board for Plant Genetic Resources (IBPGR) hosted by FAO.

From a marginalised and low-profile position, IPGRI found itself suddenly in the middle of a heated and highly politicised confrontation of economic interests over PGR on a global scale and had to modify its scope and management as a result. The previously fractious relationship with FAO had been transformed into one of close cooperation and one that acknowledged shared interests and objectives. The IPGRI developed a close partnership with FAO in preparing for the 1996 Leipzig Conference and as partners, FAO and IPGRI can share credit for the preparation of two landmark documents adopted at Leipzig: the *State of the World Report on PGRFA,* and the *Global Plan of Action.* In conjunction with the CBD and Agenda 21, these documents provide the context and course of action for the following years. At that time, IPGRI Management also succeeded in forging a productive relationship with the NGO community active in the debate.

The status and credibility of the FAO process had badly needed a boost, but in finally gaining policy control of the CGIAR gene collections, the FAO had made the breakthrough required to maintain momentum and broad support from the NGOs and Southern interests. It gave the governments meeting in Rome a sense of urgency about the issue and galvanized the Leipzig process that was to follow.

The individual CGIAR centres signed identical agreements with the FAO in 1994 placing collections of plant germ-plasm under the auspices of the FAO and agreeing to *'hold the designated germplasm in trust for the benefit of the international community, in particular the developing countries in accordance with the International Undertaking on Plant Genetic Resources and the terms and conditions set out in this Agreement'*.

The agreements established the CGIAR seed and gene banks as the only internationally recognized collections and set out a formal link between the CGIARs and their collections and the FAO's IU. These PGRFA collections continue to be the most widely used sources of *ex situ* material, and their value and relevance increases as the CGIAR continues its research into and characterization of the collections.

2.5 Intensive Negotiation Period (1997–2001)

Prior to 1997, the emphasis of CBD had been on national sovereignty rather than the global governance of genetic resources for food and agriculture. The purpose of the negotiations that followed, however, was to identify an agreement which would allow pooled sovereignty for food and agriculture (Brush 2003).

At this time the exchange of germ-plasm was moving towards a bilateral system, so countries of origin and plant breeders were drawing up their own agreements and systems of access and benefit sharing. This trend would have threatened the principle of open exchange. However, given that many commercial varieties depend on material from several sources, often spanning national borders, the transaction costs were becoming prohibitive for the industry. In short, the plant breeding industry required an alternative approach to access.

In parallel, there was now increasingly strong evidence that developing countries were becoming more dependent on receiving genetic material and new commercially produced varieties from other countries (Fowler et al, 2001). The demand for some form of multilateral framework for PGRFA pushed the negotiations forward.

In 1995, the second Conference of the Parties to the CDB ended the reluctance of some countries to accept the FAO rather than the CBD as the relevant negotiating forum for the revised IU because of its decision II-15 (Jakarta, 1995) *'recognising the special nature of agricultural biodiversity , its distinctive characteristics and problems, which require specific solutions'*.[3] Nevertheless, negotiations on the revision of the IU moved very slowly prior to the accession to the Chair of the negotiations of Ambassador Fernando Gerbasi of Venezuela in 1996. Highly respected in both North and South, he flexibly adopted the 'Contact Group' methodology, in which small-groups negotiators would have intense discussions and report progress to the main negotiating process. This period saw important discussions and networking occurring in parallel to the formal FAO process. For example, the UK government and the EU both hosted open discussions with European and Southern stakeholders. Key to the process were several non-government individuals who helped facilitate constructive dialogue between the CSOs and government.

The UK was active in developing the EU position on PGRFA and the potential Treaty. Work in Brussels and throughout negotiations had a very significant impact. The UK, the EU and the Nordic countries searched for pragmatic and flexible approaches and held a series of informal sessions to discuss core topics, e.g. Commercial Benefit Sharing, held at the Kew Royal Botanic Gardens, UK, in 1999. In this setting, the papers were in digestible formats and were tools to elicit debate and promote further work. The overall process and the gruelling contact group sessions between EU and G77 worked to gradually build the level of trust, resulting in a more proactive and informal role by G77. The UK, EU and G77 nexus was crucial, and the consensus forged on Farmers' Rights (FRs) during the UK Presidency of the EU in 1997–98 resulted in what became Article 9 of the Treaty on Farmers' Rights – the first article to be agreed.

It is widely acknowledged that the crucial breakthrough in establishing negotiating momentum occurred off-stage at an informal meeting of the Friends of the Chair (experts supporting the Chair's deliberations and reporting) in Montreux, January 1999. The 'Chairman's Elements' were drafted in only 15 minutes, but the four core areas highlighted formed the basis of all future Treaty negotiations (Stannard, Interview). According to Andree Sontot, the lead French negotiator, *'Montreux really had an impact. It was clearly, carefully and transparently organized, the preparation was through the formal diplomatic process, involving the Chair, Secretary and EU. It identified a basis to move forward. The existing text was not useable - it was a total mixture, with no structure or guiding principles'.*

The Chairman's Elements stipulated the need for a multilateral system covering an agreed list of crops selected on the basis of food security, interdependence and the collections of the IARCs. Facilitated access to this system would be allowed to minimize transaction costs, but would be restricted to food and agriculture use. Any benefit sharing, it was agreed, could include the transfer of technology, capacity building, the exchange of information and direct funding, but should primarily benefit farmers' interests in the developing countries. Crucially, the Chairman's Elements called for the recognition of the contribution of farmers to the conservation and development of PGR and declared that the responsibility for realizing Farmers' Rights should rest with national governments and supporting national legislation.

2.6 Farmers' Rights

As indicated above, the compromise on Farmer's Rights was already in place when the Chairman's Elements were drafted. The British were influential in brokering this deal, since negotiations took place during the UK Presidency of EU in 1987–8. Chairing key negotiating sessions, Linda Brown of DFID, acting on behalf of the EU, was central in driving through the deal on Farmers' Rights that set the framework for the final text (Martin Smith, Interview). This legacy is of lasting controversy within the alliance of progressive Northern players, CSOs and Southern negotiators.

> *'The only real trade off was our acceptance (I have been criticised for it; I thought it was the best thing we could do) of an American offer that Farmers' Rights could be recognized by law but at the national level. For international law to recognize Farmers' Rights would mean that the US would be bound by this; they would never accept this and the confrontation would never stop. Global recognition of national legislation on farmers' rights allows us to defend what is ours.'*

> (Tewolde Egziabher, Interview)

> *'On Farmers Rights, the concession was outrageous, it was a mistake. Jan Borring, Cary Fowler, and Rene Salazar were there inside the closed meeting. They told me "We*

think something terrible has happened". I wrote an analysis saying that it was a disaster. It wasn't too late because Philippines and Poland were still consulting with capitals. The concession was made far too soon - there were too few of us, we weren't applying enough pressure. I ranted and raved with Tewolde to no avail.'

(Pat Mooney, Interview)

Thus, whilst the NGO and FRs lobby have criticized what they see as undue emphasis on the nation state at the expense of a globally consistent system of rights, some representatives of the South have defended their decision to compromise with Northern interests on this issue. The African Group thought it necessary to submit to the US offer of national level responsibility because of what it viewed as a total impasse (the US was unlikely to sign up to international systems that protected the rights of specific socio-economic groups in other nations). Many representatives of the South saw this as a necessary concession in order to be able to defend FRs nationally in the face of foreign challenges.

However, the NGOs that strongly believed that FRs should be central to any fair management system for PGRFA felt that Southern delegates had surrendered their case to the North much too early. Their concern was that this would fundamentally undermine the significance and usefulness of the Treaty.

Finally, there are those who remain totally dedicated to protecting the world's PGRFA heritage from aggressive commercial interests but who see the entire concept of FRs as essentially flawed. As a distinguished and long-term campaigner against commercial appropriation of PGRFA, Erna Bennett has also criticized what she sees as a compromise position of 'negotiating with the robber' by the NGOs that attempted to represent the South during the discussions. This strategy, argues Bennett, legitimizes the entire IPR system and can only lead to 'conceptual chaos', since indigenous forms of stewardship are meant to merge with post-industrial and formal legal systems [see Montecinos (1996) and Bennett (2002)].[4]

2.7 The List

With complex technical issues to be negotiated by diplomatic representatives, there arose a process of commissioning research in tandem with particular negotiating topics in order to identify and make accessible the options for prioritizing and classifying PGRFA for a non-scientific audience. In this case the CPRGFA played very detailed attention to promoting as wide a list of crops as possible to be placed into a multilateral system by the countries from which these crops originated. The decision on whether or not maize varieties should be added to a multilateral germplasm exchange system would fall to Mexico, even though the development of maize as a crop long pre-dated the formation of the modern Mexican state.

Clive Stannard, of the CGRFA Secretariat, identified some key elements of the research that encouraged countries and negotiating blocs to pool their genetic resources.

'Important research was tabled at a conference of the Instituto Ultramare in Florence in October 1998, hosted by the Italian Ministry of Foreign Affairs. The Secretariat requested this from the Italian government, which was very supportive of a favourable outcome to the negotiations. The strategy was to find technical descriptors to make a list based upon 'interdependence' and 'food security'. This was worked out between the Commission and IPGRI. The paper presented by Toby Hodgkins of IPGRI very carefully laid out options rather than prescriptions. It was a very successful meeting attended by key diplomats and technical experts. A paper by J. Robinson and L. t'Mannetje

widened the scope of the discussion by dealing with crops, fodders and pasturages. This research was a way of opening up the discussion in 2001. It allowed governments to see the units they were dealing with and gave them the confidence to cut out or not cut out species of particular relevance. It provided a technical basis on which to work and opened up the possibilities for detailed negotiations.

'Highly respected and excellent scientists conducted crucial technical work at a crucial point. It gave tools to negotiate and courage to broaden out from species to the gene pool level. The research was done at a sufficient distance from the negotiations. For example, technical experts from the Vavilov Institute in St. Petersburg provided technical underpinning for the Treaty with their work on wheat, showing that the gene pool for wheat is wider than a single species. It opened up the understanding of the need to talk about crop gene pools and not plant genus.

'The Transaction Cost Paper was also vital looking at consequences of country-by-country negotiations. Bert Visser (head of the Dutch genebank) led the paper on transaction costs of bilateralism. It was presented at a meeting of the Global Forum on Agricultural Research in Dresden in 2000. Technically, it was the best set of papers, came out of very mature understandings developed by Cary Fowler and Carlos Correa. It brought out their best contributions at a time of greatest concern that an agreement would never be reached. Together, these papers provided the technical basis upon which governments could negotiate the inclusion or omission of crop groups.'

(Clive Stannard, Interview)

Despite providing options, the research could not eliminate the uncertainties due to the 'chicken and egg' nature of the problem, characterized by Geoff Hawtin: *'How can we know what we want to put into the system until we know what it is? How can we design the system if we don't know what's in it?'* (Hawtin, Interview).

Many Southern stakeholders saw the final list as a breakthrough in its own right, but the reality is that many locally important crops in the South were omitted from the list (Tewolde Egziabher, Interview). Despite the very careful planning of useful research contributions, the strategy nearly unravelled completely in the final negotiation sessions in the autumn of 2001. The negotiations became ensnared in a process in which crops became bargaining chips and were added or dropped on national and political grounds. Mexico and Peru excluded certain sub-species of maize. The proscribed and inflexible negotiating position of some countries, in particular China and Brazil, was seen by some as a major disappointment; it seemed to represent a lack of understanding of the purpose of any list and the value of multilateral sharing (Hawtin, Interview).

2.8 Commercial Benefit Sharing

The basis of agreement in this area of negotiations was a paper by ASSINSEL (now the International Seed Federation), the international body representing the private plant breeding industry, and the interest group at the centre of the treaty provisions in this area. It adopted a formal *'Position on access to plant genetic resources for food and agriculture and the equitable sharing of benefits arising from their use'* at its General Assembly in June 1998 and distributed this position at the CGRFA's negotiating session the same month. It stated that *'in the event of protection through patents, limiting free access to the new genetic resource, ASSINSEL members are prepared to study a system in which the owners of the patents would contribute to a fund established for collecting, maintaining, evaluating and enhancing genetic resources'.*

The negotiations which followed are described by Pat Mooney.

'Negotiations on this issue were taken forward to Neuchatel, Switzerland, for a Contact Group Meeting. The ASSINSEL Formulation, which was picked up by Norway and Japan, accepted monetary benefit sharing for new varieties commercialized from germplasm material exchanged under the provisions of the treaty. The United States position was that patenting is a globally acceptable form of benefit sharing, which makes innovations available but also protects intellectual property rights. The US strong-armed the Japanese in Tokyo for its representatives at the Neuchatel meeting to desist from promoting monetary benefit sharing. Then Jan Borring, the Norwegian negotiator, took charge of the work. This went forward to Tehran for a five-hour meeting to define commercial benefit sharing language, but the US bracketed it.'[5]

(Mooney, Interview)

Critical voices were also raised about the ASSINSEL Formulation from CSOs on the legitimation and entrenchment of intellectual property rights.

'On the surface, it might seem like a fair thing to do: to ensure that part of the profits that the North makes on the South's germplasm flow back to the South. But there is a lethal trap built into this scheme. Money will only come out of it if all countries accept the principle of IPRs on life. The more patenting, industry says, the more financial benefit. The countries that are echoing this position in the IU negotiations are actually advocating a strategy that will reduce access to biodiversity for everybody. This defeats the very objective of the IU. What is often forgotten in the FAO talks is that by allowing – promoting, in fact – the patenting of crop germplasm covered by the IU, a steadily increasing flow of valuable material will actually leave the multilateral system to become the private intellectual property of a few powerful corporations. This is the very gene-drain from the public to the private sectors that the IU negotiations are meant to reverse.'

(The IU, Time to Draw the Line on IPRs, Seedling, March 2001)

With sympathy for the CSO view prevailing amongst experienced Southern lead negotiators such as Tewolde Eghabiazar (Ethiopia) and Rene Salazar (Philippines), it was very difficult to see where the breakthrough might come, but intense negotiations in the final sessions did produce a formulation acceptable to all parties.

'The final breakthrough came right at the death. The crucial breakthrough is that monetary benefit sharing is triggered by commercialization. There is no mention whatsoever in the text of intellectual property mechanisms. The US could not accept a binding interpretation of its patent system at the international level, but they were happy to accept benefit sharing on the results or outcomes of an IPR system.'

(Mooney, Interview)

Some CSOs and policy influencers, such as RAFI, were successful in publicizing the issues and shaping the direction of the Treaty negotiations with carefully judged material. RAFI developed two key documents, termed 'translators', specifically intended to provide accessible overviews of the issues and outline national and international options both before the signing of the Treaty (*'Frequently Unasked Questions about the International Undertaking on Plant Genetic Resources'*, March/April 2001, RAFI Communiqué 69), and after (*'The Law of the Seed'*, December 2001). The former encapsulated the delicate balance required on benefit sharing within a multilateral system of access to germ-plasm, defending the importance of reaching agreement in light of the more uncompromising positions outlined above (Box 6).

Box 6. Civil Society's Final Demands. (adapted from 'Frequently Unasked Questions About the International Undertaking on Plant Genetic Resources', March/April 2001, RAFI Communiqué, Issue 69).

CSO positions in the final stages of the negotiations as presented by Pat Mooney, a participant in Contact Group discussions at the invitation of the Chair (RAFI, 2001).

Q. Who benefits from a multilateral system?
A. Poor and poor countries with finite research and genebank resources.

Q. Facilitated access – why bother?
A. Without an agreement, exchange barriers will rise, the CGIAR will be unable to monitor, financial support will decline for agricultural research programmes, exotic germplasm free flow will end.

Q. Commercial benefit sharing?
A. There is a profound disconnect between value of agricultural biodiversity and the North's willingness to pay. But how do you set up a payment system when the cumulative value is incalculable but the actual value in any single year could be negligible. Industry should sever the patent connection and pay a percentage of their annual profits associated with crops that are part of the MLS

Q. CGIAR, benefit or beneficiary?
A. Just because the South uses a greater volume of gene bank materials does not necessarily mean that they benefit more. With more material to hand and more sophisticated labs the north/companies can cherry pick IARC genebanks.

Along similar lines, a significant mobilization by a global coalition of civil society organizations took place leading up to the Contact Group Meeting in Spoleto, Italy, at the end of April 2001, with over 100 organizations signing a statement of support of the NGO contact members inside the negotiations. This was based on coordinating efforts by Patrick Mulvany through the UK Food Group web resource www.ukabc.org, which worked during the negotiations to broaden the basis of awareness of the critical negotiation issues amongst civil society organizations. This included a CSO position paper, 'Seeds for All' (www.ukabc.org/iu.pdf), issued in 2000, which emphasized elements that the Treaty needed to include in order to conserve agricultural biodiversity and ensure long-term food security.

Once the negotiations were concluded, CSOs and other groups defending the interests of farmers welcomed several of the Treaty's declarations on benefit sharing. In particular, the statement that monetary benefit sharing should be triggered by commercialization placed the onus on the plant breeding industry to compensate donors of PGRFA and acknowledged the right of farmers to freely utilize these resources.

Andersen (2006a) has reviewed the attitudes to the two alternative approaches to monetary benefit sharing: 1) the allocation of profits from sales relating to farmers' varieties or 2) the provision of general funds to farmers proactive in the *in situ* maintenance of PGRFA. Northern stakeholders tend to stress monetary incentives to conserve PGRFA, whilst Southern stakeholders place greater emphasis on mechanisms to feed back profits from sales.

A summary of the key decisions and agreements within the five transition stages is presented in Figure 2.

Figure 2. Summary of Key Decisions and Agreements

1983 - FAO Conference adopts International Undertaking (IU)
       - Establishment of the Commission on Plant Genetic Resources (CPGR)
1989 - FAO Resolution 4/89 states plant breeders' rights not inconsistent with IU
       - FAO Resolution 5/89 recognizes Farmers' Rights
1991 - FAO Resolution 3/91 recognizes sovereign rights of nations to their genetic resources
1992 - Agenda 21 (Chapter 14 - SARD) at UNCED Rio calls for strengthening of the FAO Global System on plant genetic resources
1993 - Convention on Biological Diversity (CBD) enters into force
1994 - First Extraordinary Session of CPGR starts revision of IU to harmonize it with CBD
1995 - CPGR's mandate expands to make it the Commission on (all) Genetic Resources for Food and Agriculture (CGFRA)
1996 - FAO Leipzig International Technical Conference on plant genetic resources, where 150 countries adopt the Leipzig Declaration and the Global Plan of Action
2001 - Sixth Contact Group Meeting (Spoleto), followed by 6th Extraordinary Session of the FAO Commission on Genetic Resources for Food and Agriculture, 25-30 June 2001, Rome, of CGFRA adopts revised IU (July)
2001 - FAO Council considers pending issues on IU and IT PGRFA adopted by the FAO Conference (November)
2004 - ITPGRFA comes into force (June)

Notes

1 Malcolm Gladwell (2000) has given us the useful concept of the *Tipping Point* to describe major social changes apparently brought about by a very small group of individuals who are particularly astute at interpreting and acting upon social trends. One example is a sudden and dramatic world-wide surge in demand for a particular product.

2 The resistance to funding arrangements by the North forced the CGRFA to abandon a discussion of financial mechanisms at the Leipzig Technical Conference and prompted the FAO to avoid a debate on budget issues at the World Food Summit.

3 UNEP/CBD/COP/2/19 Decision II/15.

4 Erna Bennett was at the forefront of a movement in the 1960s and 1970s that forced the urgent need to research, document and protect the world's PGRFA into the public domain. *'Plant Introduction and Genetic Conservation: Genecological aspects of an urgent world problem'* (1965) and *'Genetic Resources in Plants'* (Frankel & Bennett, 1970) helped raise the profile of the issue and attract international support for global conservation programmes for PGRFA. As the privatization of PGRFA accelerated, she became increasingly concerned about the power exerted by vested interests over issues meant to address global governance of these resources. She spent 15 years at the FAO before resigning in 1982 in the face of increasing corporate interference and influence, but continues to write and lecture on the issues.

5 In UN negotiations, if text is bracketed that means that it is not yet agreed.

3

The Treaty and its ratification

The International Treaty on Plant Genetic Resources for Food and Agriculture (the Seed Treaty) was eventually adopted at the 31st session of the FAO Conference on 3 November 2001. Seven years after Resolution 7/93 called for the revision of the IU in line with the CBD, the CGRFA had finally achieved a tangible breakthrough and legally binding agreement. The culmination of years of difficult and sometimes fraught negotiations involving some 180 countries, representatives of plant breeding and biotechnology companies and NGOs, the International Seed Treaty represented a huge advance from the non-binding IU of 1983. Crucially, the Treaty appeared to reconcile the CBD's emphasis on national sovereignty of genetic resources with the concept of 'common heritage' and a global legal system for shared access to PGRFA.

The Treaty was approved by 116 countries, with only the United States and Japan abstaining, apparently due to ambiguity over intellectual property rights (Fowler, 2003). The US later signed the Treaty in November 2002, five months after the EU had signed, but it has not ratified it.

The Seed Treaty was intended to complement the CBD with an acceptable and workable global framework for sharing *in situ* and *ex situ* PGRFA that recognizes Farmers' Rights and, by developing a multilateral system of access (MSA) to a list of crop genera and fodder species important for global food security, the Treaty complemented the CBD by adding a formal structure that also addressed social and economic aspects of the biodiversity of agricultural plants.

The structure of the Treaty is simple and is shaped by three sections: *General Provisions* (Articles 4-8); *Farmers' Rights* (Article 9); and the *Multilateral System of Access and Benefit-Sharing* (Articles 10-13).

The *General Provisions* apply to all PGRFA and call for all contracting parties to adopt an integrated approach to the exploration, conservation and sustainable use of these resources. This includes the collection of new material, the support of farmers' systems of conservation and the role of *ex situ* collections. These themes and the focus on national obligation are consistent with the CBD and the GPA.

The article on *Farmers' Rights* requires the parties to recognize the contribution of farmers and communities in the conservation and development of PGFRA, but rather side-steps full responsibility by granting this task to governments. '*[E]ach Contracting Party should, as appropriate, and subject to its national legislation, take measures to protect and promote Farmers' Rights.*' The text is quite explicit that the Treaty not be interpreted in such a way that would remove existing rights to save and exchange farm-saved material but, nonetheless, the onus for securing these rights is passed to the national level (see Section 3.2).

The *Multilateral System of Access and Benefit Sharing* is centred on the set of crop and forage genera listed in Annex 1, apparently selected on the basis of significance to food security and interdependence. The list contains 35 genera of crops and 29 forage species, but not all these are automatically included within the MSA. The Treaty states that the MSA shall include all PGRFA within the list that '*are under the management and control of the Contracting Parties and in the public domain*'.

Several industrial crops with existing commercial and bilateral agreements are omitted from the list as a result. As Cooper (2002) states, the omitted crops include rubber, coffee and tea, but also crops with obvious food security roles, such as groundnuts, oil-palm, soybean, cassava, sugar, cane tomato, peppers and onions.

Part V of the Treaty, *Supporting Components*, outlines activities external, but essential, to the Treaty. It calls for the increasing implementation of the Leipzig GPA and the establishment of an effective Global Information System on PGRFA. The significance of the IARCs in this sharing is acknowledged, and the MSA requires they sign agreements with the Governing Body to grant access to all Annex 1 material held in their collections (the subject of Article 15). The Treaty does not identify other *'relevant international institutions'* by name, however.

Part VI of the Treaty, *Financial Provisions*, requests the Contracting Parties to help establish a transparent and predictable funding strategy that ensures that benefits from commercialization are reinvested in the MSA and that programmes and plans within the Treaty are sufficiently supported.

Finally, the *Institutional Provisions* set out the structure and role of the Governing Body, which is to be comprised of all members and is to guide the implementation of the Treaty by consensus. The Secretary of the Governing Body is to be appointed by the GB itself.

3.1 The significance of the Treaty – stakeholder perspectives

The principal architects of the Treaty would agree that a key achievement has been to stress that rational governance of PGRFA must be a truly global effort, and that bilateralism cannot work to secure fair and sustainable use of these vital resources, given the interdependence of countries for PGRFA. However, there is also an acknowledgement that the Treaty has merely set the ground rules for a mandatory multilateral system, and that the next stage is to establish the architecture and mechanism for benefit sharing (Hawtin, Interview).

How will the IT PGRFA manifest itself? Fowler (2003b) believes that the flow of germ-plasm will become freer and more routine than before and that material received from the multilateral system (e.g. in the form of seed) will remain available for use in that form, even if the isolated and purified form has been patented. Intellectual property rights will still have a role, according to Fowler, and the Treaty may even allow for US style patent protection for parts and components (genes) of varieties.

It is possible, however, that freeing up the system of exchange may reduce the funds available for the global management of PGRFA, and Brush (2003) questions whether revenues raised as a direct result of commercialization will be sufficient to support conservation efforts. Whilst Southern stakeholders are pleased with the Treaty's commitment to benefit sharing from commercialization, there is widely held concern that these mechanisms will not be effectively enforced. It will be important that commercial interests are properly monitored by independent agencies or watchdogs.

Publicizing infringements of the benefit sharing principle and using case studies as examples of good and bad practice may be useful tools to promote transparent benefit sharing by the industry (Tewolde Egziabher, Interview). In addition, many feel that in excluding IPRs from the benefit sharing mechanism, the South will be short-changed, and that ideally all benefits from commercialization should somehow go to a central fund.

Whilst there is consensus in the South that the Treaty represents a step in the right direction, there are also serious concerns over how the Treaty will be implemented and how the various trade offs, implicit in the Treaty, will be contested.

The capacity of countries to operate and negotiate within this new system might well remain as uneven as it was before. The capacity of national legislative frameworks to control access and benefit sharing and to balance conservation with facilitated access will be crucial (Andrew Mushita, Interview). There are other challenges that might lie beyond the scope of national governments, and there is still scepticism from the private sector about the practicalities of the Treaty and how gene banks might realistically track the use of their collections in commercial products (see, for instance, Charles, 2001).

Finally, respondents were keen that the multilateral system of access be quickly implemented and that the language of the Treaty be converted to a practical and workable system of transfers. In this respect the Treaty must offer the research establishment something that the CBD fails to deliver (Arturo Martinez, Interview).

3.2 The multilateral system of access

3.2.1 The List

Despite the commissioned research and scientific knowledge of interdependence, origin and nutritional value, the eventual list was largely a political compromise.

'In practice the list, set out in Annex 1 to the Treaty, was negotiated at least in part on the basis of the perceived interests of individual negotiating parties, with some crops important to food security excluded.' (Moore & Tymowski, 2005).

Some country negotiators appeared to misunderstand or misrepresent the purpose and significance of the global list and applied a rather aggressive approach to adding or removing certain crops according to perceived national interest. The conventional indicator for crop importance (a function of global or regional production and the contribution to human dietary intake) was evidently not the only influencing factor here. In particular, plant genera with important, but often non-market, roles for the poor in the developing world were poorly represented. Cooper (2002) suggests that the list does not represent the real significance of many African forage grasses and Latin American forage legumes, with only 29 of the world's 18,000 forage species included. In addition, there are conspicuous gaps in commercially significant food crops, with soybean, cassava, groundnuts and sugar cane missing from the list. Other obvious omissions include tomato, soybean, peppers, onions and sugar cane.

The uncertainty surrounding the implications of the list – how the list will be used to permit access and how this might impact on national economic interests – impelled Brazil, China, India and others to withhold important food crops and forages. The implication here, completely contradicting the spirit of the Treaty, is that bilateral agreements would better meet national interests. The strategy might also imply that extra genera might be added at some later date, depending on the performance and impact of the Treaty.

The scope and coverage of the list obviously had to be tempered by practical considerations of length if it were to be meaningful and workable, and Cooper (2002) believes that the list does in fact distil the basis of PGRFA of global significance. Although local varieties and weed species may play crucial roles in providing food security, the list does include those genera where access is required internationally. The suggested list ranged from 6 to 400 crops (Moore & Tymowski,

2005), and, given that the negotiating countries varied so widely in their opinion of desirable size and composition, the list does represent something of a consensus.

It is unclear what process will be followed when the origins of varieties and their status with respect to the list are contested by the contracting parties.

3.2.2 Benefit sharing

There are several key declarations in the Treaty with respect to the scope and mechanism for sharing. Firstly, the MSA is intended to make only important food related material available for use, research, and conservation, and explicitly excludes material with pharmaceutical or other industrial uses. Crucially, material is to be shared for the Treaty's purpose, but not to enable exclusive ownership through intellectual property rights in law. However, the extent to which the Treaty actually prevents the privatization of PGRFA and its benefits remains a salient area of debate. Those concerned with biopiracy and the increasing power of international biotechnology interests were not comforted by the following: '*Recipients shall not claim any intellectual property or other rights that limit the facilitated access to the plant genetic resources for food and agriculture, or their genetic parts or components, <u>in the form received</u> from the Multilateral System*' (footnote ref 12.3.d, emphasis added). It remains to be seen how viable this aspect of the Treaty is in relation to a growing emphasis on the patent in agricultural research and development and the continuing influence of UPOV and PBRs.

The Treaty is generally not specific on the institutional identity of prospective donors and recipients.

One of the most important sections of the Treaty and the MSA is Article 13, which outlines the range and purpose of the sharing of PGFRA and its benefits. The Contracting Parties are required to:

1) make available all information relating to inventories, research results and technological processes associated with the plants listed in Annex 1;
2) provide access to and transfer of technologies such as improved varieties derived from the list '*whilst respecting applicable property rights and access laws*';
3) establish programmes for research, training and education related to the conservation and sustainable use of PGFRA, particularly in developed countries; and
4) facilitate commercial benefit sharing through the Treaty's MTA, whereby a proportion of the benefits arising are contributed to a central mechanism. This will be in line with the beneficiary's ability to pay, but the major recipients of benefits must remain farmers, especially those in developing countries.

In this last regard, the Treaty's statement that '*benefits accruing* [from PGRFA] *shall be shared fairly and equitably...*' is backed by a requirement that commercial beneficiaries of PGFRA pay into some form of fund supported by the Governing Body. This is seen by many as a fundamental right of farmers and nation states, as custodians of agricultural diversity, to enjoy the benefits of its use and modification through research and development.

3.3 Farmers' Rights

The complexity of the Treaty, as well as any discussion of its impact and value, is compounded by the difficulty of 1) making crucial genetic resources universally available and 2) ensuring that the custodians of these resources are properly acknowledged or in some way benefited.

Although the FAO had earlier adopted a resolution on FRs at the 1989 Confer-ence, the controversy that followed took up much of the negotiation time in the formulation of the IT PGRFA (Cooper, 2002). Some have argued that the politicization of the negotiation process for the CBD and the Treaty, and its focus on issues of sovereignty and local rights in developing countries, actually threat-ened the overriding objective of global food security and PGRFA conservation.

The issue of FRs was central to the development of the Treaty. As farmers became increasingly more isolated from their own sources of food and income, the issue attracted a range of dedicated CSOs, NGOs and individuals to build global aware-ness and keep FRs at the core of the FAO discussions.

The negotiations that led to the International Undertaking and that eventually paved the way for the IT PGRFA did much to put the concept of FRs in the public domain. Advocates of greater farmer representation and power from the South such as GRAIN and the African Group publicized the historic and continuing role of farming communities in maintaining and enhancing genetic diversity, and the Rural Advancement Foundation International perhaps did most to popularize the term 'Farmers' Rights' and promote it as a major policy issue in the mid-1980s.

The Treaty directly acknowledges the role of farmers in the sustainable use and management of PGRFA. '*Contracting parties recognize the enormous contribution that the local and indigenous communities of all regions of the world...have made and will continue to make for the conservation and development of plant genetic resources which constitute the basis of food and agriculture production throughout the world.*'

However, the Treaty does not confront directly the issue of ownership and con-trol. Rather, national governments are requested to ensure that 1) traditional knowl-edge is protected, 2) farmers are entitled to share in the benefits of the utilization of PGRFA and 3) farmers have the right to participate in decision-making at the national level.

Although these final provisions are non-specific, Cooper (2002) considers the second point, the new right to share benefits, to be one of the most fundamental and significant parts of the entire Treaty. This is the first time that farmer-specific rights to the fruits of technical and biological innovations of PGRFA have been expressed in international law, and it could have a positive effect on halting in-creasing concentration of ownership and control.

Equally significant is the right to participate in decision-making. Acknowledg-ing a role for farmers in national level decision-making is an important first step, and it is hoped that farmers will play a proactive role in the implementation of related activities, such as the Global Plan of Action. However, if the governance of the world's PGRFA is to be truly democratic and representative of the range of interests in both the developed and the developing world, new channels for farmer participation will need to be encouraged (see 'Putting the Treaty's FRs directives into practice' below).

There has been steady growth in the emergence of national and international networks representing FRs and the interests of producers, both in the North and the South. The political autonomy of these groups adds gravitas to their demands and avoids the criticism levelled at some NGOs that they were merely representing a Northern and idealized version of what the South might really want and require.

Article 9 of the Treaty lists the provisions with direct relevance to FRs. However, the essence of the IT PGRFA is to provide a framework for the management of PGRFA that will conserve diversity and maintain access, and this ensures that FRs-related issues are touched on throughout the Treaty. The *General Provisions* express the right of farmers to participate in the management of PGRFA, for instance, and this is echoed in the *Multilateral System of Access and Benefit Sharing*.

The significance of the Treaty to FRs remains hotly contested. Some, but not all, of the groups that had lobbied on FRs issues felt angered by an apparent lack of commitment, the ambiguous terminology and the lack of any internationally binding commitments. Crucially, the Treaty is neutral on the issue of 'farmer's privilege' – the right of farmers to save, use and exchange or sell seed (Moore and Tymowski, 2005). Concessions were made in order to achieve international consensus, and in particular to gain the signature of the United States, but relegating the formal recognition of FRs from a global to a national obligation has been very controversial. While it provided the opportunity for countries to set standards and defend farmers' interests against external threats, it placed a huge responsibility on countries to develop and enact supportive policy and law.[1]

However, many others felt that the Treaty marked a significant breakthrough by shifting the attention to farmers' issues and establishing the foundations for serious negotiations on benefit sharing. What is generally agreed is that the Treaty has defined a new space for more purposeful discussion and negotiation. FRs are directly or indirectly linked with many of the unresolved issues of PGRFA and their management, and the Treaty has acknowledged this.

The Treaty has shifted the emphasis from technical innovation and commercialization to fair use and food security for the vulnerable. The Treaty will not neatly resolve unfair and discriminatory PGRFA practices, but it will at the very least set a framework for future negotiations.

3.3.1 Putting the Treaty's FRs directives into practice

Opinion on the potential of the Treaty to protect and develop FRs remains split. While the ambiguity of the language and its emphasis on national responsibility are seen by many as weaknesses, other PGRFA stakeholders value the moral message and legal backing that the Treaty represents and that the Governing Body now advocates.

The Governing Body has commissioned *The Farmers' Rights Project* to develop a common understanding of the issue and to help inform strategies to implement the Treaty's provisions.[2] The first phase of the project has yielded some interesting suggestions, and perhaps the most essential is the call to agree a consistent working definition of FRs for the Governing Body and the parties to the Treaty. This will help in the process of sharing experiences and the evaluation of success. Andersen (2006b) proposes a working definition and warns that too great a discrepancy in the interpretation of FRs and implementation without proper understanding of overarching objectives could cause more problems for farmers than it solves.

> *'Farmers' rights consist of the customary rights that farmers have had as stewards of agro-biodiversity since the dawn of agriculture to save, grow, share, develop and maintain plant varieties, of their legitimate right to be rewarded and supported for their contribution to the global pool of genetic resources as well as to the development of commercial varieties of plants, and to participate in decision making on issues that may affect these rights.'*

A survey undertaken by *The Farmers' Rights Project* revealed that although of greater concern to developing world stakeholders, awareness of FRs issues is increasing in the North in parallel with the growing interest in sustainability and the right to refuse the cultivation of GM varieties (Andersen, 2005). Farmer demand for the right to save and manage seed appears to be growing stronger in the North.

A major challenge is converting the FRs provisions (and the language used) in the Treaty to the reality of poor farmers in the developing world. This would make farmers and others better aware of their rights and their potential contribution as custodians and innovators. Unfortunately, most of the concepts of ownership in the Treaty are totally alien to the local level systems of plant and animal husbandry that emphasize sharing in order to minimize risk. As Bennett (2006) states, *'those whose forebears created the genetic wealth that is so greatly desired by the wealthy and their powerful corporations find the concept of property a quite foreign one. Their view is that we are the custodians of nature and its wealth, but it is not our property'*.

In many cases, the management of seed and other plant resources may relate more to the maintenance of social cohesion or to insurance against seasonal hardship or shocks, such as drought or flood, than it does to the financial benefits of exclusive ownership.

> *'The local property rights on PGRFA and related knowledge (in Peru) have been developed by people who may not have worked with traditional farmers. Traditional knowledge is part of a very complex culture and registering it is equally complicated in addition to being a strange concept. We are going to try it out with a first catalogue of Huancavelica potato varieties. Nevertheless, the varieties are available in many other communities and we believe that these new concepts of "owners of knowledge" go against their culture, in which seeds are to be shared and not owned.'*

(Maria Mayer de Scurrah, Grupo Yanapai, Peru, cited in Andersen, 2005)

Promoting the participation of farmers in the management of PGRFA will be a struggle in developing countries. National policy frequently defines the need for input from local producers and other stakeholders in the management of agriculture, fisheries and forests, but the reality is often disappointing. Although national policy tends not to translate to widespread support of smaller farmers' interests, the number and range of success stories in both the developing and the developed world imply huge potential for formalizing or supporting such initiatives and scaling up in the future (Andersen, 2005).

There seems to be broad consensus that the most pressing FRs issues involve reliable access to PGRFA. The survey by Andersen suggests that this overarching right is perceived as far more important than potential mechanisms of monetary benefit sharing or the establishment of participatory plant breeding, for instance. Rather, the priority should be to maintain access to PGRFA, to protect farmers' knowledge and promote farmer participation in PGRFA decision-making.

Many of the obstacles to realizing FRs and to ensuring continued access can broadly be termed 'institutional' and are constraints that hamper drives for change and development more generally, both in the North and the South (Box 7). Case studies collected from Asia, Africa, South America and Europe suggest that these constraints are global (see Andersen 2006b), but the appropriate strategy to support FRs will differ with context. In the developed world, legislation to restrict the capacity of farmers to save or sell seed may already exist. In contrast, most developing countries will not have such legislation, and it is important that laws support, rather than hinder, these rights as expressed, albeit neutrally, in the Treaty.

Andersen's survey suggests a key priority should be identifying mechanisms to promote the sharing of resources among farmers, NGOs and governments. This would go a long way to publicizing the concepts, the threats to the vulnerable, and new roles for government or civil society.

Although complex systems of benefit sharing or compensation do not appear attractive to the majority of PGRFA stakeholders, it may be possible to establish

Box 7. Obstacles to realizing FRs (adapted from Andersen, 2005).

- **Lack of awareness of FRs**
  Limited knowledge of what FRs encapsulate – within formal authorities, CSO facilitators and the farmer communities themselves. New networks of farmers and their representatives may promote FRs and awareness.

- **Economic and political factors**
  Economies of scale and other market forces undermine small-scale farmers whilst agriculture agencies are emphasising intellectual property rights at the expense of collective or local initiatives.

- **Inadequate legislation, policy and implementation**
  Many countries either do not promote a political/planning role for farmers or cannot enact suitable policy to do so.

- **External factors**
  International organisations such as WTO, UPOV and the IMF and private interests such as the commercial plant breeders continue to promote intellectual property rights and can challenge FRs policy.

- **The quality of representation**
  Whilst many national and international organisations continue to lobby for FRs, many CSOs may lack the capacity to influence policy makers. Training in advocacy may be an option.

- **The real meaning of the Treaty**
  The Treaty is perceived by many as non-committal or ambiguous on FRs but the language used has ensured some agreement on the way forward. Discussions on mechanisms to share the financial benefits from PGRFA are now under way, for instance.

incentives for good practice. This would encourage innovation in FRs policy and practice and help promote success stories when and where they occur.

A major question remaining is how the PGRFA stakeholders should combine to implement the Treaty's FRs declarations. Although the Treaty places the emphasis at the national level, Andersen (2006) highlights the key role to be played by the Governing Body. What role should the Governing Body provide, and how should it articulate with national governments, NGOs, breeders, civil society and farmers? The *Farmers' Rights Project* revealed demand for a range of alternative structures (Figure 3), but perhaps more important was the potential role and approach of the Governing Body. The survey revealed broad agreement that the Governing body

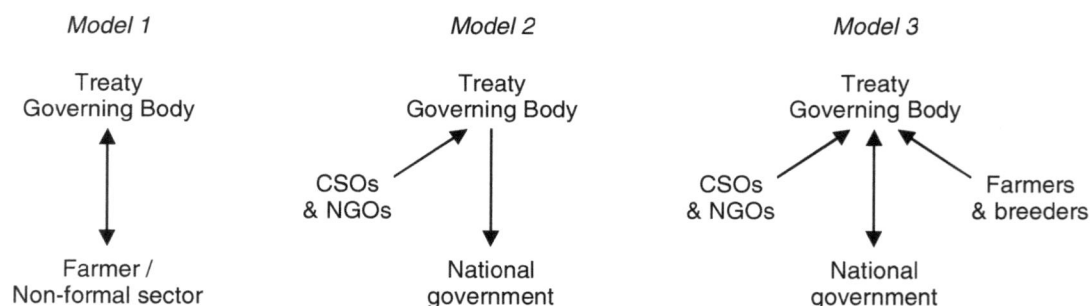

Figure 3. Some alternative institutional arrangements for the promotion of FRs. Model 1 is unrealistic given the Treaty's emphasis on national government responsibility. Model 2 lacks direct participation by farmers and perhaps represents the past approaches of Northern and Southern NGOs during the negotiation of the Treaty. Model 3 accommodates direct contact between farmers and the Governing Body but acknowledges a potential role for commercial plant breeders (developed from Andersen, 2005).

should facilitate the sharing of experience, and that this could be done by the development of national level plans to promote FRs. In turn, these plans could form the basis of performance monitoring and encouragement by the Governing Body.

To date, the political arguments surrounding the concepts of FRs and how to achieve them can be reduced to two main approaches: the ownership approach and the stewardship approach (Andersen 2006b). Broadly, the former has been championed by proponents of formal mechanisms of ownership and IPRs for PGRFA that would attempt to compensate farmers for commercial benefits derived from farmers' fields. In this context, FRs might comprise the ability of farmers to secure fair deals on mutually acceptable terms or the ability to participate in the formulation of IPR policy.

However, those most active in the area of FRs have stressed a stewardship approach whereby farmers are given the political space to retain traditional or local practices. The emphasis is on food security and *in situ* conservation of PGRFA. In addition, as Andersen (2006b) notes, the emphasis now is less on preventing the unfair extraction of PGRFA by plant breeders than on ensuring the maintenance of diversity in the field. In addition, the ownership approach has not yet proved that it can properly accommodate local forms of PGRFA management that rely on sharing and seed saving, for example (see Mooney and Mulvany, 2006).[3]

3.3.2 Summary

The *Farmers' Rights Project* suggests a much more proactive role for the Governing Body. There is little doubt that there is inadequate guidance and support at international and national levels, and Andersen (2006b) recommends that the Governing Body establish a working group with the specific task of planning and implementing a strategy to enact Article 9. In parallel, NGOs and donors still have much to do to promote FRs issues at the national level and to act as facilitators in developing farmer participation in decision-making. Greater awareness of FRs is required at ground level.

As new threats to genetic diversity and viability appear, support for FRs must allow the politically marginalized to react in ways which maintain their independence and their livelihoods. FRs would incorporate the capacity to challenge the uncontrolled distribution of GM food aid or the uptake of GURTs, for instance.

In addition, it is crucial that Parties acknowledge the role of women in global agricultural and as custodians and users of PGRFA. Genetic erosion and technological changes threaten the social and economic role and contribution of women in agriculture. The Seed Treaty does not acknowledge this role (unlike CBD and GPA), and there should be more attention given to the impact of the Treaty on women and the political space for women to contribute in debate and implementation, i.e. through participatory plant breeding. The Convention on the Elimination of All Forms of Discrimination Against Women (CEDAW), adopted in 1979 and comprising 176 Parties, could provide the basis to ensure the Treaty is fully inclusive and non-discriminatory, but little has been done to date to implement the Convention and influence national or international programmes relating to PGRFA (FAO, 2004).

Finally, any discussion of FRs must acknowledge the vulnerability of the world's poor and the obstacles they face in realizing political influence or voice. Farmers in the developing world may struggle to secure access to food, potable water, adequate health support and political representation, and these constraints are common to the whole range of rural and urban stakeholders in the South. Consolidating FRs may require providing a political space for participation and inclusion that few nations currently provide. In this regard, FRs in the context of development should not be seen as distinct from citizen's rights and the broader objective of improved governance and social development.

It seems that raising awareness of rights to farmers and others, and discussing what these rights may actually look like, is a crucial task on the way to consolidating FRs.[4]

Notes

1 The issue is complicated by many Southern governments having poor records on rights and the issue being pushed by Northern NGOs.

2 'The Farmers' Rights Project is an international project set up at the Fridtjof Nansen Institute in Norway with the support from the Norwegian Ministry of Foreign Affairs and the German GTZ, with affiliated experts in Peru, India and Ethiopia, to facilitate such a common understanding and develop a basis for proposals to the Governing Body of the IT PGRFA on specific measures to be taken'" (Andersen 2006b)

3 Although there appears to be an underlying conflict between these approaches, Ethiopia has recently developed policies that attempt to reconcile aspects of both IPRs and a stewardship approach (Andersen, 2006b). It remains to be seen how successfully such policy can be enacted.

4 This could create demand for change from below. The UK Department for International Development has applied a 'Drivers of Change' (DoC) model for tapping into the energy and political influence of civil society and NGO advocates of pro-poor development. The DoC model centres on the potential of individuals and organizations to influence institutions and policy. To some degree, this assumes an environment receptive to change and the existence of a 'social contract' between the state and its constituents, with demand driven from below and services provided by government in order to maintain its legitimacy and public support.

4

Key factors in the PGRFA policy process

4.1 Analysing the evolution of the Treaty and the contribution of research

4.1.1 The analytical framework and methodology

While there is extensive literature on the research-policy links in OECD countries, from disciplines as varied as economics, political science, sociology, anthropology, international relations and management, there has been much less emphasis on research-policy links in developing countries. The massive diversity of cultural, economic, and political contexts makes it especially difficult to draw valid generalizations and lessons from previous experience.

Traditionally, the link between research and policy has been viewed as linear, whereby a set of research findings is shifted from the 'research sphere' to the 'policy sphere', where it then has a direct impact on policy-makers' decisions. At least three of the assumptions underpinning this traditional view are now being questioned. First, the assumption that research influences policy in a one-way process (the linear model); second, the assumption that there is a clear divide between researchers and policy-makers (the two communities model); and third, the assumption that the production of knowledge is confined to a set of specific findings (the positivistic model).

Analysis of the research-policy link is now shifting away from these assumptions, towards a more dynamic and complex view that emphasizes a two-way process between research and policy shaped by multiple relations and reservoirs of knowledge (e.g. Garrett and Islam, 1998; RAWOO, 2001).

The Research and Policy in Development (RAPID) programme of the Overseas Development Institute (ODI) aims to better understand how research can contribute to pro-poor policies, aiming to improve the use of research and evidence in development policy and practice. RAPID has developed a framework for assessing how research influences policy that breaks down the policy process by considering 1) the political context, 2) the credibility of the research and evidence and 3) the links between policy and research communities.[1]

4.1.2 Context

The links between research and policy are shaped by events and trends in the wider political context. Political agendas, power relations and institutional pressures are aspects of the policy process. The policy context is also governed by a dominant set of ideas variously referred to as a discourse, a paradigm or a narrative, which exerts a powerful influence over which ideas are considered and which are ignored. Major change in policy usually follows the establishment of a 'counter narrative', which enables previously marginalized views and voices to gain legitimacy.

4.1.3 Evidence

The degree of attention paid to circulating ideas is, to an extent, dependent upon the skills, ingenuity and timing of their backers. Whether an idea elicits an engaged response from actors depends upon a range of factors, such as the perceived credibility of the source, the way in which it is communicated and the language used.

4.1.4 Links

The research policy link is played out in the interface between the political context and the actors involved: networks, organizations and institutions, and individuals. Actors may interact through official policy working groups or through more informal networks.

The RAPID framework has proven itself a very useful analytical tool, not necessarily to rank context, evidence and links in terms of their importance, but to look at each of them in turn as different facets of the same process in order to bring important, realistic insights, particularly for civil society activists and researchers, into the scope and nature of the influence they might expect to have in global negotiation processes.

4.2 The role of the political and institutional context (setting)

In the early 1980s the South's demands in relation to agricultural genetic resources were for free access, no intellectual property rights and political control through a multilateral framework and forum. But the political winds began to change. The privatization of agricultural research in industrialized countries was propelled by neo-liberal policies and developments in technology. Patenting gained acceptance. The South then opted for a radical change of strategy – national sovereignty and fair and equitable sharing of benefits. The alliance between NGOs and Southern governments began to fracture as more complex coalitions emerged.

Negotiations at Rome also felt the impact of the strengthening of the UPOV Convention in 1991. It introduced the category of 'essentially derived variety' from an existing protected variety. The grant of a PBR (plant breeder's right) on this category became dependent upon the authorization of the original breeder. This reduced the flow of scientific information between the private and public sectors; the private sector was not interested in having public competitors who develop varieties for public welfare. It also created temptations for market orientation of public sector research institutes in times of scarce public funding. This has become a source of increasing acrimony between CGIAR scientists and functionaries and NGOs.

Growing international concern about the environment was accompanied by growing expectations of the future value of biodiversity, which rose with each stunning prediction and breakthrough from the emerging biotechnology industry. US court cases and administrative rulings opened the path to the patenting of seeds.

Developed countries continued to emphasize full guaranteed access to genetic resources and their need for guaranteed benefit sharing. Few actors were stressing the need for both. Indian and US researchers were professionally close, but Indian scientists advocated farmers' rights and an international fund and were vocal critics of the US patent office. Brazil was happy to accept a multilateral system as long as its scope was limited to materials that Brazil lacks, and as long as the benefit sharing agreement did not prejudice or set a bad precedent for non-agricultural genetic resources

Due to the close relationship of the CBD and the WTO, the resolution of critical issues eluded negotiators in both forums. Negotiators did not have the authority to make meaningful compromises. Some specific PGRFA cases, in both North and South, had little or no access to the upper echelons of government bureaucracies that would have sufficient authority to make rulings. Sector-based, day-to-day political agendas cannot contend with the complexity of genetic resources management.

The growth of private sector investment in crop breeding research has increased the total utilization of genetic resources, but a new regime harmoniously combining the relative contributions of the private and public sectors has not yet emerged. The presence and rapid expansion of IPRs in relation to biological materials led to a charged atmosphere in FAO-CBD negotiations. The US, with a huge capacity to produce new knowledge, has continually pushed to increase the realm and clout of IPRs. For Kenya, on the other hand, the value of natural resources should be recognized and compensated for by those who use them.

From the late 1990s the context changed further, with the primacy of trade issues. Only a last-gasp intervention by Ethiopia (Tewolde Egziabher) at the WSSD in 2002 prevented the agreement of a final text subordinating all environmental treaties to trade considerations. Many developing countries were prepared to go along with this. One factor was the increasing suspicion by these countries of the civil society environmental movement in the North, which was proposing measures whose net outcome would be the restriction of opportunities for economic development in the short term. Another factor was heavy bilateral pressure on developing countries from the US and EU to respect the free market model as the basis of the international order. This created a much more complex and difficult terrain for NGOs, and Northern NGOs in particular.

In addition, trade has become a more attractive issue for the South, which can now go on the offensive against Northern subsidies. However, in the case of conservation of genetic resources, the main avenue for resources for the South will be donor aid. This provides little potential to challenge the global status quo. Moreover, the aid will target poor and remote farming regions rather than prestige projects and will bring a host of potential entanglements and conditionalities.

4.3 The role of research and knowledge ('evidence')

Up to the early 1990s independent lobbyists and researchers could volunteer evidence at meetings on the International Undertaking. From 1994, Commission Secretariat staff members anticipated sticking points and commissioned the research necessary to achieve progress. This happened because the process became formal and inter-governmental when it entered into the negotiations for a binding UN treaty.

Country negotiators were constantly briefed by the CGRFA on the findings of research commissioned on key and poorly understood issues. As the account of the negotiations (Section 2.5) showed, this research was closely controlled by the CGRFA, using highly credible researchers. Northern negotiators tended to be less dependent on these papers, having their own national sources of scientific advice, but were supportive of the role of IPGRI. Civil society position papers did not have significant impact on the negotiations at this stage.

'The most useful research was by stakeholders in the process. It was preferable if it was handled by IPGRI, or a similar institute directly involved in core activity under discussion. These "empirical studies with a purpose" were easier to use in the process of negotiations. Government delegations don't know how to use a contribution from an advocacy group.'

(Andrée Sontot, Interview)

From Southern negotiators' perspective the commissioned research was very helpful, but no substitute for top class negotiating skills.

'The role of these research papers was to break the log-jam, and it worked. The Africa Group delegation members were desperate for expertise. There was a need for information in order to mount statistically back arguments. But no amount of statistical preparation can help after 15 hours of negotiations at 3am. The art of negotiation is to come up with the language that enables you to defend your position. It is a poker game. So the outcomes were determined not so much by factual issues, but by the craftiness and skills of the Northern negotiators, who wrapped us up in flowery language which seemed to mean what we wanted but proved to be empty of any legally binding commitment.

'The Africa Group needs a crafty team. We should not always be reacting. So many principles have been lost. You need good research and crafty negotiators – it's not either/or.'

(Andrew Mushita, Interview)

Looking at the impact of a single piece of research in more depth has revealed the symbolic role of research rather than the usefulness of the detailed scientific argument involved. The example selected is CGRFA Background Study Paper No.7, 1999, *Contribution to the estimation of countries' interdependence in the area of plant genetic resources* (Ximena Flores Palacios, Environmental Economist, Consultant to Bolivian Ministry of Sustainable Development).

As the negotiations intensified, the papers produced were pressed into more immediate political use. The interdependence paper is often cited as one of the key consensus building inputs. Research on interdependence was planned in three stages: centres of origin, secondary centres and gene banks. It was, on the part of Ximena Flores, a search for scientific answers. Strong caveats were placed around the first paper on centres of origin, which could only be meaningful if backed up with the other two studies and in-depth country case studies. In fact, the paper on primary centres, which was completed by the beginning of 1998, proved to be the only paper on the theme. As a research consultant, Ximena Flores did not follow the process through and was not aware of the political significance of the work (Flores, Interview). For her it was a technical research brief. It was very useful for those within the process to call on respected scientific experts in order to legitimate headline political messages. In an interview, the CGRFA Director José Esquinas stated that

'In the agriculture sector not a single country is self-sufficient. Each country needs, on average, 70% of its genetic resources from other countries'.

(Interview at www.oepm.es)

This might be taken to imply that we are constantly returning to the centres of genetic origin of wheat to maintain bread production. It is at this point that Esquinas turns to an historical moral obligation of the developed countries.

'The problem is not only technical, but also political. With reference to the potato famine, Europe was the most developed continent and its problem was solved thanks to the contribution of one of the poorest. It was genes from Peru, Bolivia and Ecuador that solved the problem. Therefore, there is a need to transform a moral obligation into a legal obligation.'

This emphasis on the country of origin in constructing arguments around inter-dependence has been criticized from various perspectives.

'The interdependence paper was focused upon species and not on genetic resources. The issue of domestication vis-à-vis creation of varieties was not touched. Therefore the paper was detrimental to understanding. The question of country of origin was not good for the process – it was totally detrimental.'

(Andrée Sontot, Interview)

'Material in gene banks is now extinct in situ due to genetic erosion. It is important to examine modern germ-plasm transfers and see what can be learned from them...important to construct a legal system that addresses contemporary issues and not those of a bygone age that no longer exists.'

(Fowler, 2003a)

Nevertheless the Interdependence paper *did* achieve its political purpose of bringing home the message that *'the world is interdependent on Genetic Resources, so national sovereignty is not relevant'*. Arguments put forward were simplified and caricatured versions of the science, but they opened up negotiation possibilities by creating the right climate for countries to agree to put the universal use of genetic resources on the table.

Basing arguments for interdependence purely on primary centres of origin is technically flawed because countries become less interdependent if they can use secondary centres and gene banks. Without this oversimplification, however, African and Latin American blocs may not have agreed to the List.

4.4 The role of linkages

Linkages forged between NGOs and representatives of Southern governments at the FAO in the early 1980s were of lasting significance, giving certain respected individuals from civil society a role of considerable influence throughout the IU and Treaty negotiations.

The 1980s were the heyday of this collaboration. For example, in 1985, when the Commission first met, Farmers' Rights were immediately brought forward, with Mexican support. The Dutch created an uproar by saying that FRs were impractical and utopian. This played into the hands of the NGOs, who could strengthen their credibility by denouncing the Dutch statement. At the same meeting, RAFI was briefed to the effect that the IBPGR was pulling out of Rome in order to escape the control of the FAO. As observers at the FAO, RAFI were deliberately unguarded and revealed the results of a private meeting at which the IPBGR's plans were discussed, something that official delegates would never have done (Mooney, Interview).

Commission staff were also seen as champions of the cause of the South, and the creation of the Commission was viewed as an achievement for progressive developing country thinking, a bridgehead in the UN system. But at the same time, they were able to bring the US to the table for the Keystone discussions. The tradition of off-the-record informal contact sessions was maintained throughout the decade.

Box 8. NGO support for the Africa Group

'The Africa Group, was involved in the CBD and COPs which affected the revision of the IU, and became involved in negotiations on the revisions of the International Undertaking in 1996. The Africa Group had already started a similar process of negotiation on biosafety, and the same technique was applied in both sets of negotiations; to consult within Africans nations and arrive at a common position, identify the positions on specific issues to be submitted, and then before each meeting to go through all the submissions make comments analyse them in the context of what is of importance to Africa, and distribute our comment before hand to that all the African delegations knew of it.

The Africa Group often had just one day to arrive at a consensus. It was supported by a number of UK NGOs, notably the Gaia Foundation and ITDG. With Gaia this included raising the funds for the additional one-day preparatory meetings. The Gaia foundation was very valuable to us. Within Africa it was difficult to communicate internally. It proved easier to send a draft negotiating position to London, and Gaia would get it out. Just finding an airline ticket for one person here one person there – that made a lot of difference to us. The UK NGOs and the Africa Group spent a lot of time on basis logistics: trying to identify who were "good people", trying to get them connected in their countries, get them invited by the FAO, making sure they know that the invitation is coming. Then they worked on organising the meeting before hand and making sure they had the right paper.'

(Tewolde Egziabher, Interview)

Although governments were now setting the agenda, they could not achieve the desired involvement of the seed industry without also involving NGOs. In 2000, negotiations were rekindled through a contact group in New York in which Pat Mooney used his linkages with Don Duvick (Pioneer Seed Corporation) and US negotiator Henry Shands. The combined voice of industry and NGOs softened the US position (Mooney, Interview). The process featured long-term commitment by a number of protagonists representing different interests who were locked into the process at every stage and knew, understood and respected each others' positions. Apart from this, there was crossover from civil society into official roles, with David Cooper and Cary Fowler moving into the FAO at key moments and maintaining close linkages with NGOs.

With negotiations in full swing at the FAO, the NGOs developed a new supportive and less protagonistic role, which nevertheless had a vital impact in levelling the playing field for Southern negotiators and Southern networks such as the Africa Group (Box 8).

4.5 Summary

The ITPGRFA was achieved through more than 20 years of concerted effort from a wide range of stakeholders and interests. The negotiations were highly complex because they fell at the interface of a variety of constantly changing governance processes in agriculture, environment, trade and intellectual property rights. Existing institutions like WIPO and UPOV and international agreements such as TRIPs and CBD had to be accommodated and represented. The issues of FRs and national sovereignty for the South further diversified the range of interests, positions and coalitions of the parties, and new, well-organized voices emerged to represent the interests of civil society and farmers in both the North and South.

The ITPGRFA policy process was fed by commissioned and independent research, with 14 official background papers and hundreds of position papers developed in an attempt to inform or influence the course of the negotiations. The most influential research was produced by, or in conjunction with, actors already inside the process. These individuals were already well-respected and known to the prominent players, and the issues they tackled were recognized as crucial but unresolved themes by others in the negotiations. The publications of the Northern NGOs and think tanks were highly influential in the early stages of the PGR negotiations.

Rather than simply being annexed to negotiating papers, these research papers were shared and discussed in a series of informal inter-sessional meetings, supported by a range of Northern countries and donors. These sessions worked to build understanding between the main protagonists in the process: Northern governments, Southern governments, the private seed sector and civil society organizations.

Although a few key individuals from these NGOs continued as insiders from start to finish, their opportunities to influence the course of events narrowed over time. It is questionable whether Northern NGOs and individuals will be able to do this in the future, but there can be a role for Southern civil society organizations and farmers' movements in filling the political space once occupied by Northern entities. NGOs also were supportive in raising funds and creating capacity building opportunities for African government representatives and non-government observers. It is this latter role in the implementation and future negotiation of treaty related issues that international NGOs can continue to play.

Note

1 The framework is based on an extensive literature review (de Vibe, Hovland and Young, 2002), conceptual synthesis (Crewe and Young, 2002) and testing in research projects (Court and Young, 2003; Court and Young, 2004). For information on RAPID research and practical projects, see www.odi.org.uk/rapid

5

Continuing threats to genetic diversity and the Seed Treaty's objectives

5.1 Threats from new biotechnology

The capacity of the plant breeding industry to capture and then prevent, by biological means, the re-use of the genetic components and traits of plant varieties is increasing. If left unregulated and unchallenged, this will have a profound impact on access to genetic diversity, food security and FRs. The dangers are greatest in the developing world, where approximately 1.4 billion farmers and their families are reliant on a vast array of varieties and seed management practices, and where legal and regulatory structures may be insufficient to detect or block the use of this technology.

Of particular concern are genetically modified varieties that block the farmer's capacity to produce agronomically viable seed, ensuring that farmers will have to buy new seed each season, thereby tying them to future purchases of inputs. These Genetic Use Restriction Technologies (GURTs) can dramatically reduce the germination of farm-saved seeds (v-GURTs) or produce plants in which other key traits are expressed on exposure to specific environmental or chemical triggers (t-GURTs). It is the so-called 'terminator technology' of the v-GURTs, in particular, which threatens continual access to and farmer development of the world's PGRFA heritage. In this regard, GURTs represent a considerable threat to the Treaty and any concerted global effort to manage the world's agricultural genetic heritage.

Campaign and advocacy groups such as the Action Group on Erosion, Technology and Concentration (ETC Group; formerly RAFI) and GRAIN have published detailed critiques of the risks, and routinely provide updates on biotechnology industry developments and strategies. In parallel, farmer and peasant movements, like Via Campesina (Box 9), and national and international CSO networks have lobbied on a massive scale to ban GURTs.[1]

Their concerns are echoed in the official stance of the parties to the CBD and IT PGRFA, which have called for further research and analysis of the potential impact on FRs and food security and the need for a precautionary approach that will keep GURTs away from farming systems. On 31 March 2006, the CBD re-affirmed its *de facto* moratorium on the field testing and commercialization of GURTs and

---

Box 9. Via Campesina. International network of Peasant and Farmers' movements.

Via Campesina (The International Peasant Movement) has encapsulated the professional and dedicated effort of this movement and the power gained from networking and campaigning en masse. Since April 1992 Via Campesina has represented large numbers of small to medium peasant and farmers' organisations in Asia, America, Africa and Europe and has fought to protect the rights of indigenous communities, women and poor farmers in the face of corporate threats to farming practice and sustainability. Its remit extends beyond agriculture, seeking to promote rural development and social justice and to ensure that the poor are properly accommodated within the decision-making process. (Ref www.viacampesina.org)

opposed the efforts of Australia, Canada and New Zealand to lobby for a case-by-case approach to risk assessment. Had these countries been successful in overturning the moratorium, it is likely that this would have opened the way for field trials in some countries (see www.banterminator.org).[2]

The risks associated with GURTs are interrelated, but essentially concern 1) appropriation, ownership and control of access and use of seeds and 2) Farmer's Rights, local practices and food security.

5.2 Appropriation, ownership and control of access and use

GURTs directly challenge existing systems that regulate IPRs by patents or PBRs. Plant Breeders' Rights permit novel cultivars to be protected, but these restrictions are bound in time and space, i.e. this monopoly privilege can be reviewed, is time-limited, and is presently subject to the principle of territoriality, so can operate locally. GURTs represent a fundamental challenge to this system because ownership is achieved through technological means (the production of sterile seed), rather than legal means. Ownership can be established without recourse to expensive legal processes and in settings where IPR institutions are lacking, such as the developing world. In contrast to the patent system, given the uncertainty over uptake and ecological impact (below), it is possible that once a foothold for GURTs is established, the spread of reduced germination of seeds and fertility of plants will be difficult or impossible to reverse.

The system of IPRs for PGRFA, as represented by UPOV, is not without its limitations with respect to FRs (it recognizes FRs as a 'privilege' that may or may not be conferred by governments) or the spirit of the Treaty, but it does allow governments an element of control and the capacity to direct research and development in those areas most suited to national needs.

Attempts to patent GURTs themselves could be challenged with recourse to existing international instruments.[3]

5.3 Farmer's Rights, local practice and food security

GURTs directly challenge the Seed Treaty's key provisions on FRs under Articles 9.2(a), 9.2(b), 9.2(c) and 9.3.

The ability to protect traditional knowledge [Article 9.2(a)] would be undermined because PGRFA is traditionally managed and developed through systems of seed saving and exchange relevant to local livelihoods and conditions. This traditional knowledge and practice would be undermined by GURT varieties that induce sterility, especially if these varieties were to spread into adjacent areas through aggressive marketing or cross-contamination.

The potential to equitably participate in sharing benefits arising from PRGFA (Article 9.2(b)) is threatened because GURTs provide a means to appropriate the world's genetic heritage without the accountability afforded by conventional IPRs. This might mean that local strains are, in effect, annexed and isolated from the original beneficiaries and custodians of the varieties. Commercial benefits would be accruable only to the developer of the GURTs.

'As an appropriation method ("restriction use"), GURTs might not provide for a balance of societal and individual benefits that intellectual property systems do. Contrary to other legal intellectual property systems such as those derived from the International Convention for the Protection of New Varieties of Plants (UPOV), patent and other rights mechanisms such as provided for in the International Treaty on Plant Genetic

Resources for Food and Agriculture and the Convention on Biological Diversity, GURTs do not make available the new varieties or traits for further breeding.'

(UNEP/CBD/SBSTTA/9/INF/6-UNEP/CBD/WG8J/3/INF/2)

GURTs would erode the capacity for community innovation and reduce the participation of farmers in equitable management of PGRFA. With respect to Article 9.2(c) and the right to participate in national decision-making relating to PGRFA, the complexity of the development process of GURTs will not accommodate input by farmers as the ultimate end users. The information and decision-making associated with GURTs will stay exclusive to the commercial breeders, whilst the terms and conditions of their use will pass the burden of responsibility on to farmers (Box 10).

Finally, the right to save, use and exchange seed (Article 9.3) is deliberately and utterly undermined by V-GURTs. However, Article 9.3 qualifies this by adding the phrase *'subject to national law and as appropriate'*. Thus, if the government determines that farmers should not have the right to save seed, the seed and plant-breeding companies could successfully argue that v-GURTS could be a way of implementing this ruling.

Despite serious concerns about the economic, social and environmental impact of GURTs, these technologies continue to be developed and patented. To date their transboundary movement as GMOs is formally restricted by signatories to the Cartagena Protocol on Biosafety under the CBD and, in principle, by the FAO Code of Conduct on Biotechnology as it affects genetic resources for food and agriculture. Crucially, however, the ability to withstand this technology ultimately rests with national capacity to regulate and challenge the industry and, as Mulvany (2001) states *'strengthened legislation including liability and redress, use of TRIPs Article 27.2 and improved labelling of GM products would be more effective'*. It is crucial that this regulatory capacity is developed as soon as possible, in line with Article 8 (Technical Assistance) of the Treaty.

5.4 Threats to livestock

The genetic erosion of livestock, in both the North and South, is perhaps exceeding that of plants. Livestock breeds that have co-evolved with communities for centuries are being lost, as a narrow range of breeds and systems of husbandry are promoted and adopted. Over 7000 breeds have been developed from about 40 do-

---

Box 10. Technology use agreements for GM growers.

Technology use agreements force farmers to shoulder responsibility in return for the right to grow GM crops:

- *Liability Limits*: Farmers who sign technology agreements limit the liability of the GM manufacturer with respect to losses, injury or damage that result from the use or handling of a product containing the gene technology.
- *Right of Venue*: Right of venue clauses allow the seed company to force breach of contract disputes arising from technology agreements to be settled in court jurisdictions favourable to the corporation and costly to the farmer.
- *Dictate Farming Conditions*: Some technology agreements stipulate that the producer has responsibility for ensuring that pollen from his or her GM crop does not trespass on a neighbour's crop.
- *Post-Harvest Liability*: Agreements may require farmers to prevent contamination of export channels or food chains with GM grain – placing still greater responsibility on the farmer.

(Adapted from GRAIN [2004] Interview, Hope Shand, *Seedling*, April)

mesticated species (Scherf, 2000), but many have recently become extinct, while a still greater number are now endangered. Of 5330 breeds of livestock mammals, for instance, 17% are now extinct and 29% are endangered (Geerlings et al, 2002, cited in Köhler-Rollefson, I. 2004). The globalization of animal production is a principal cause (State of the World's Animal Genetic Resources, FAO, 2006).

In many parts of the developing world, pastoralists had developed complex livelihoods that had minimized threats to survival and maintained year-round access to food or income. The diversity of breeds had also performed important social functions, and current trends in husbandry and ownership have, in many cases, introduced new conflict and caused serious ecological problems. In addition, these new systems often require additional, externally sourced, inputs of cereal feeds and veterinary supplies.

The monopolization of animal genetic resources is perhaps more extreme than that found with plants, with a small number of very large companies aggressively consolidating vertical integration into farm feeds and other supplies (Gura and Köhler-Rollefson 2006).

As with PGRFA in the development context, livestock genetic diversity is bound up with rural development, livelihoods, food security and the capacity to practice customary forms of husbandry and exchange. The issue of Livestock Keepers' Rights touches upon all these issues and is a major concern for those who have called for greater effort to conserve this genetic heritage.[4]

Securing the rights of livestock keepers to continue a diverse range of livelihood strategies will help maintain genetic diversity and guard against genetic dilution from newly developed breeds, including genetically modified animals.

In making FRs a central component of the IT PGRFA, the FAO has probably gone a long way in legitimizing the issue of Livestock Keepers' Rights. Declarations such as the Karen Commitment have helped build on this momentum. They call for an equivalent international agreement that complies with the CBD and champions the rights of the stewards of these resources (Box 11).

The Karen Commitment also raises issues that should be addressed by the FAO's draft Code of Conduct on Biotechnology, developing this Code to include issues concerning the possible genetic modification of livestock.

We call on governments and relevant international bodies to commit themselves to the formal recognition of the historical and current contribution of pastoralists and pastoralism to food and livelihood security, environmental services and domestic animal diversity.

The FAO Global Strategy for the Management of Farm Animal Genetic Resources was initiated in 1993 with the specific goal of halting the erosion of these resources and working towards sustainable use. The Global Strategy consists of four basic components:

- an intergovernmental support mechanism to enable direct government involvement and ensure continuity of policy advice;
- a technical programme of interdependent activities to characterize, use, develop and conserve those irreplaceable resources;
- a geographically distributed and country-based structure, supported by regional and global focal points, to assist national actions; and
- a reporting component to aid planning and to monitor and evaluate progress (CGRFA, 2004).

The initiative has broad political support, and at least 130 countries have nominated National Coordinators for animal genetic resources in an attempt to establish national networks and provide feedback to the FAO (the Global Focal Point).

Box 11. The Karen Commitment – Pastoralist/Indigenous Livestock Keepers' Rights. The statement was developed by leaders of traditional livestock and pastoral communities, government representatives, CSOs with a focus on livestock genetic resources, academics and livestock researchers, Karen, Kenya, 27-30 October 2003.

We also demand that they recognise the contributions of pastoralists and other livestock keepers, over millennia, to the conservation and sustainable use of animal genetic resources for food and agriculture including associated species and the genes they contain (AnGRFA).

Furthermore, we insist that there is international legally-binding recognition of inalienable Livestock Keepers' Rights and the Rights of their communities to:

* continue to use their knowledge concerning the conservation and sustain-able use of AnGRFA, without fears of its appropriation
* participate democratically in making decisions on matters related to the conservation and sustainable use of AnGRFA
* access, save, use, exchange, sell their AnGRFA, unrestricted by Intellectual Property Rights (IPRs) and [modification through] genetic engineering tech-nologies that we believe will disrupt the integrity of these genetic resources
* have their breeds recognised as products of their communities and Indigenous Knowledge and therefore remain in the public domain
* benefit equitably from the use of AnGRFA in their own communities and by others.

We call on the Food and Agriculture Organisation of the UN (FAO) to start negotiating such a legally-binding agreement, without delay, ensuring that it will be in harmony with the Convention on Biological Diversity. We further call on the FAO to develop a Global Plan for the conservation and sustainable use of AnGRFA by pastoralists, other livestock keeping communities and relevant public institutions.

Finally, we insist that AnGRFA be excluded from Intellectual Property Rights claims and that there should be a moratorium on the release of genetically-modified livestock until bio-safety is proven, in accordance with the Precautionary Principle. We call on relevant institutions concerned with food, agriculture, trade, intellectual property and animal research to provide assurances and such legal protection as is necessary to sustain the free flow and integrity of AnGRFA, vital to global food security and the environment.

Source: www.ukabc.org/karen.htm

However, it appears that the Strategy needs to develop channels for fuller community participation if it is to be better understood by stakeholders outside the technical and scientific community. This may increase its legitimacy and impact.

In summary, there is little doubt that the issue of animal genetic resources for food and agriculture has attracted less public and expert attention than PGRFA. One of the constraints on highlighting the severity of the threat has been the difficulty of establishing the economic value of these resources. It is the diversity itself that has greatest value to mankind and local societies, not a capacity to generate commercial products. Most conventional evaluation cannot sufficiently recognize these environmental and cultural or social functions. Influencing the way in which countries view and analyse these agricultural resources, incorporating participatory methods and a greater qualitative appreciation of farming communities, for instance, will increase their perceived value and promote the issue of genetic conservation nationally (Drucker, 2004).

Notes

1 See, for instance, '*Who calls the shots at UPOV? US Government and Multinational Seed Industry Force UPOV to Abandon Critique of Terminator*', Genotypes, 17 April 2003, ETC Group (2003), http://www.grain.org/publications/ and http://www.viacampesina.org/main_en/index.php?option=com_content&task=blogcategory&id=22&Itemid=37

2 In the UK, the lobby successfully encouraged more than 260 MPs to sign an 'Early Day Motion' (1300) and start a debate on terminator technology in the House of Commons (8 March 2006).

3 'For patents over GURTs inventions, the question arises of whether governments might wish to investigate relevant aspects of Article 27.2 of the WTO TRIPS agreement, which enables exclusion from patentability of inventions that threaten the ordre public or morality, in order to protect human, animal or plant life or health, or avoid serious prejudice to the environment, provided that such exclusion is not merely because the exploitation is prohibited by their law. (CGRFA-9/02/17).

4 It is universally acknowledged that viable and dynamic genetic resources in livestock can only be conserved on a meaningful scale *in situ*, i.e. exposed *in vivo* to different environments on-farm or on pastoral ranges.

6
Conclusion

The governance of the world's PGRFA is of fundamental importance to humanity. Approximately 95% of food crop varieties have been lost in the last century, but the widespread use of the major global commodities (rice, maize, potatoes and wheat represent more than half the dietary energy of the world's population) and the rising influence of and monopolization by larger and fewer commercial interests provide real obstacles to sustainable and fair systems of management. Environmental threats are likely to proliferate as climate change increases the frequency of epidemics and pest outbreaks. Global warming will necessitate that agriculture draw increasingly from the diversity of the world's PGRFA heritage to help in the development by farmers of varieties suitable to new local conditions and meet new international demand. The Treaty represents a landmark effort to map out the fair and sustainable future governance of these resources.

The realization of the International Seed Treaty required more than 20 years of concerted effort from a broad range of stakeholders and interests. The negotiations were difficult and complex because they affected the interests of the institutions and individuals representing agriculture, the environment, biosafety, trade, intellectual property rights and, more recently, the concerns of the South. Established international institutions and pre-existing international agreements like TRIPs and CBD were joined by new and well coordinated networks of CSOs and NGOs and farmers' movements in both the developed and the developing worlds.

6.1 Decisive Transition Episodes

- **1981–83** *Formation of the Commission on Plant Genetic Resources for Food and Agriculture and the International Undertaking*

  The FAO adopts the International Undertaking on Plant Genetic Resources and establishes a Commission to facilitate its development. The profile of the Commission was the result of a contested vote at the 1983 FAO Conference and was opposed by several industrialized countries. At this stage, the most influential research-generated evidence was being presented in the impassioned reports of the Canadian NGO, RAFI. These contributions served to politicize and dramatically raise the profile of the genetic resources policy process. In summary, the debate on plant genetic resources and their governance had become an element of the North-South political divide.

- **1989–1991** *The Keystone Dialogues*

  A series of talks including all stakeholders in the policy process was organized by the Keystone Center, Colorado, USA. These 'Keystone Dialogues' had the desired effect of increasing understanding on the basis of mutual trust and respect amongst all relevant parties in the field of plant genetic resources for food and agriculture. The exchanges created the conditions for the US to become a Commission member in 1990. This phase in the Treaty's evolution demonstrates the key role of increasing linkage between stakeholders in the policy process. It is important to note that many of the protagonists in the Keystone Dialogues remained committed to the process throughout and brought the spirit of informal dialogue to the tough intergovernmental negotiations that lead to the adoption of the Treaty.

- *1992* *The Nairobi Final Act*

In establishing the Convention on Biological Diversity, this act recognized the specific and distinct nature of agricultural biodiversity and called upon the FAO to renegotiate the International Undertaking on Plant Genetic Resources in harmony with its provisions. This act is an example of a major change of policy pushing the process in an entirely new direction. However, the solidarities created during the Keystone Dialogues created a coalition strong enough to ensure that the specific issue of agricultural biodiversity could survive and find its place within the new global environmental agenda.

- *1993–94* *The FAO-CGIAR accord*

The status of international seed collections collected from farmers' fields and held in trust in CGIAR gene banks was established in an accord with the FAO. The perceived threat of gene bank privatization receded, and civil society commitment to the IU revision process increased as a result. The decision to make these collections accountable to the FAO was the culmination of 15 years of activism by NGOs, certain government representatives at the FAO, progressive CGRFA officials and dedicated research scientists. A continuous stream of high quality polemical papers from a handful of specialized NGOs criticizing the global governance of germ-plasm collections eventually forced the decision to bring the seed banks under the control of the FAO.

- *1997–2001* *An intensive negotiation period*

This was the comprehensive phase of intergovernmental negotiations for a binding international agreement. Commissioned research was fed into the negotiating process at strategic points, but as intergovernmental negotiations intensified, professional diplomats were sent by governments to Rome as replacements for standing representatives with scientific backgrounds. This advanced the prospect of a successful outcome, but increased the need for objective briefing of diplomats who lacked in-depth knowledge of the subject matter. It became increasingly difficult for NGOs to influence the course or the outcome of the process.

Analysis of these transition episodes reveals that the roles of the protagonists evolved to reflect the political and institutional setting. The informality of early discussions was superseded by an increasing reliance on expert national and corporate representation, as Southern interests and networks entered into an uneasy alliance with Northern NGOs. In parallel, the FAO used commissioned research to help highlight the urgent need for a workable Treaty, pre-empting the primary issues for debate and achieving additional support for its cause. This research had direct entry to the negotiations and appears to have had greater influence on the process than did informal delegations from CSOs. During this time, the CPGR and CGRFA remained supportive of Southern networks and continued to push for concrete statements on elemental issues such as Farmers' Rights.

The role of linkages and coalitions was essential to the Treaty, with complex interchanges between and among scientific, CSO, NGO and political individuals. Many persons straddled all domains, possessing the respect of the scientific community, the trust of the South and the ear of international negotiators. These voices were able to soften the stance of powerful industry interests and key signatories such as the US, Japan and Brazil.

6.2 Challenges

The IT PGRFA represents a huge step forward in agreeing a MSA for ensuring access and benefit sharing of plant genetic resources for food and agriculture and for keeping both access and benefit sharing in the public domain. This is significant in an era of increasing pressure to privatize genetic resources. The adoption of the Treaty on 3 November 2001 was a major achievement, but debate on putting the Treaty into operation, particularly with respect to sovereignty and ownership, Farmers' Rights, and systems of benefit sharing will continue. Unresolved issues within the Treaty will require the same careful consensus building and development of policy options that took place during the early negotiations. Without these, the significance of the Treaty will be undermined, and its effectiveness in managing the global agricultural genetic heritage on behalf of all interests and for future generations will be severely threatened.

The need now is for signatories to the Treaty to make clear and consistent rulings on issues or disputes concerning ownership and access. The Governing Body must demonstrate that it has the will and the capacity to enforce the Treaty, uphold the rights of farmers and ensure that the spirit of the Treaty is not compromised. Of particular concern are the ambiguity surrounding ownership and the power to keep agricultural seeds and germ-plasm in the public domain, as expressed in Article 12.3d.

> *'Recipients shall not claim any intellectual property or other rights that limit the facilitated access to the plant genetic resources for food and agriculture, or their genetic parts or components, <u>in the form received</u> from the Multilateral System;' (emphasis added).*

Some interests are interpreting the phrase *'in the form received'* to mean that IPRs can be granted if any change is made to the original stock, so it is important that the Governing Body define what changes will affect the right of ownership. This ambiguity has already been harmful to the Treaty and, for example, resulted in ASSINSEL withdrawing their support for the IU in the face of US pressure.

Many commentators, inside and outside the negotiation process, are less than optimistic about the prospects of making the Treaty workable. It is crucial that the spirit of the Treaty and its overarching goal to ensure fair access, food security and sustainability are not lost. However, as Bennett (2002) puts it, *'however enlightened legislation may be, its effectiveness depends on its social context and on how many of its provisions survive the persistent and savage amputations carried out by state administrations that serve the interests of a powerful and privileged minority'.*

In addition, there is a real danger that farmers' movements in the South, disillusioned with the rising influence of corporations in international governance processes at the FAO, CBD, WTO and WIPO, are tending to disengage from those processes, concentrating instead on grassroots capacity building. This threatens a lack of the vigorous monitoring of future processes that was hitherto a feature of the IT PGRFA policy process.

The first meeting of the Governing Body of the Treaty in Madrid, June 2006, appears to have made a breakthrough in this regard. The meeting pushed forward discussions on FRs and agreed a legally-binding standard material transfer agreement (SMTA) that will ensure that 1.1% of the sale price of seed will be channelled to an international fund for the conservation of genetic resources for agriculture (Mooney & Mulvany, 2006). The efforts here of Norway and the CSOs have kept the FR issue at the forefront of discussions and ensured that a detailed debate will take place at the second meeting of the Governing Body (to be held 11-15 June 2007 in Rome). Although the SMTA is currently opposed by Australia, Canada and the USA, it is proposed that governments may agree to regular reviews of the implementation of FRs and that farmers might present their own formal reports as part of this process. Additional issues that must be addressed include threats to the accessibility of the *ex situ* collections through the digitization of genetic databases and the potential of farmers' organizations to play a lead role in monitoring MTAs.

In summary, the Governing Body and all signatories still have much to do to make the Treaty work. Significant financial and political support is required to build the capacity for farmer participation in the decision-making process and to support farm-level conservation of PGRFA as expressed in the Leipzig Global Plan of Action. Additional relevant organizations will need to be included and their work supported by central funds. The Global Crop Diversity Trust, for instance, can play an important role in ensuring the long-term maintenance of seeds in the world's gene banks.[1]

The Treaty does represent a major breakthrough for the governance of all agricultural biodiversity, however, and it is likely that it will provide a model for other crucial genetic resources, in particular in the fight to stop the extinction of the world's livestock breeds.

Note

1 The Global Crop Diversity Trust is an international organization whose goal is to support the conservation of crop diversity over the long term. The establishment of the Trust has involved an historic and unprecedented partnership between the FAO and the 16 Future Harvest Centres of the CGIAR.

References

Andersen, R. (2005) *The Farmers' Rights project – Background Study 2: Results from an International Stakeholder Survey on Famers' Rights*, FNI Report 9/2005, The Fridtjof Nansen Institute, Lysaker, Norway.

Andersen, R. (2006a) *Famers' Rights in Norway – Background Study 6*. FNI Report 8/2006, The Fridtjof Nansen Institute, Lysaker, Norway.

Andersen, R. (2006b) *Realising Farmers' Rights under the International Treaty on Plant Genetic Resources for Food and Agriculture – Synthesis Report from the Farmers' Rights Project (Phase 1)*, FNI Report 9/2006, The Fridtjof Nansen Institute, Lysaker, Norway.

Bennett, E. (2002) 'The Summit-to-Summit Merry-go-Round', *Seedling*, July 2002, GRAIN Publications.

Bennett, E. (1965) 'Plant introduction and genetic conservation: genecological aspects of an urgent world problem'. *Scottish Pland Breeding Station Record*, 1965: 27–113.

Brush, S, (2003) *The Demise of 'Common Heritage' and Protection for Traditional Agricultural Knowledge*, paper prepared for the Conference on Biodiversity, Biotechnology and Protection of Traditional Knowledge, St Louis, MO, April 4–5 2003.

CGIAR (2004) *Report of the Fifth External Programme and Management Review of IPGRI*, CGIAR Science Council, CFIAR Secretariat, FAO.

CGRFA (2004) *Strengthening national structures for the management of farm animal genetic resources – results of a questionnaire survey*. Commission on Genetic Resources for Food and Agriculture. 10th Session, FAO, Rome, 8–12 November 2004.

Charles, D. (2001) Seeds of Discontent. *Science* 294: 772–75.

Cooper, H.D. (2002) The International treaty on Plant Genetic Resources for Food and Agriculture, *RECIEL* 11, 1.

Court, J. and Young, J. (2003) *Bridging Research and Policy: Insights from 50 Case Studies*, ODI Working Paper 213.

Court, J. and Young, J. (2004) 'Bridging Research and Policy in International Development: Context, Evidence and Links', in Boas and McNeill, eds, The Challenge of Transnational Knowledge Networks: Bridging Research and Policy in a Globalising World, Routledge, forthcoming in 2004.

Crewe, E. and Young, J. (2002) *Bridging Research and Policy: Context, Evidence and Links*, ODI Working Paper No 173, ODI, London. Available at www.odi.org.

de Vibe, M., Hovland, I. and Young, J. (2002) *Bridging Research and Policy: An Annotated Bibliography*, ODI Working Paper No 174, ODI, London. Available at www.odi.org.

Drucker, A.G. (2004) The economics of farm animal genetic resource conservation and sustainable use: why is it important and what have we learned? Commission on Genetic Resources for Food and Agriculture. Background Study Paper No. 21. FAO, Rome.

FAO (2002) *The International Treaty on Plant Genetic Resources for Food and Agriculture*.

FAO (2004) *Recognizing Gender Aspects in Agrobiodiversity Initiatives. Building on Gender, Agrobiodiversity and Local Knowledge*.

Fowler, C. (2003a) *Diversity and Protectionism Use of Genebanks, Trends and Interpretations*, Symposium on Food Security and Biodiversity, Syngenta Foundation, Berne, October.

Fowler, C. (2003b) The Status of Public and Proprietory Germplasm and Information, As Assessment of Recent Developments at FAO, *IP Strategy Today*, 7.

Fowler, C., Smale, M. and Gaiji, S. (2001) Unequal Exchange? Recent Transfers of Agricultural Resources and their Implications for Developing Countries, *Development Policy Review*, June.

Frankel, O.H. and Bennett, E. (1970) *Genetic Resources in Plants: Their Exploration and Conservation*. IBP Handbook no.11, Blackwell, Oxford.

Garret, J.L. and Islam, Y. (1998) 'Policy Research and the Policy Process: do the twain ever meet?' Gatekeeper Series no 74. International Institute for Environment and Development.

Geerlings, E., Mathias, E. and Kohler-Rollefson, I. (2002) Securing tomorrow's food. Promoting the sustainable use of farm animal genetic resources. Information for action. League for Pastoral Peoples, Ober-Ramstadt, Germany.

Gladwell, M. (2000) The Tipping Point: How Little Things Can Make a Big Difference. Little, Brown & Co, London.

GRAIN (1996) The Global Plan of Action for the Conservation and Sustainable Utilisation of Plant Genetic Resources for Food and Agriculture. GRAIN Briefing May 1996.

Köhler-Rollefson, I. (2004) Livestock keeper's rights - conserving breeds, supporting livelihoods. League for Pastoral Peoples, Ober-Ramstadt, Germany.

Martinez Gomez, F. (2002) *La Globalizacion en La Agricultura; Las negociaciones internacionales en torno al germoplasma agricola*, P y V Editores

Montecinos, C. (1996) Sui generis – a dead end alley, *Seedling,* July 1996, GRAIN Publications

Mooney, P. (1983) The Law of the Seed, Another Development and Plant Genetic Resources, *Development Dialogue*, 1-2

Mooney, P. and Mulvany, P. (2006) Bio-Battles for Food Sovereignty: will (re-) engagement in intergovernmental processes of the FAO and CBD help society resist the increasing attacks on genetic resources for food and agriculture? Paper for the IPC Working Group on GRFA, October 2006.

Mulvany, P. (2001) Comments on GURTs paper by Patrick Mulvany, ITDG. Presented to FAO Intergovernmental Working Group on Plant Genetic Resources for Food and Agriculture, 4 July 2001.

Pistorius, R. (1995) Will Material Transfer Agreements Open Pandora's Box? *Biotechnology and Development Monitor*, 24, 20–22.

RAFI (2001) Frequently Unasked Questions about the International Undertaking, *RAFI Communique*, Issue 69

Scherf, B. (2002) FAO. World watch list for domestic animal diversity. Food and Agriculture Organization, Rome.

Bibliography

Useful Web links

http://www.etcgroup.org
http://www.biodiv.org
www.ukabc.org
http://www.fao.org/AG/cgrfa/itpgr.htm
www.africanfarmdiversity.net
www.viacampesina.org

All official documents cited can be found on the CPGRFA pages of the FAO website:

www.fao.org/ag/cgrfa/default.htm

Meetings of the Commission

30 October–1 November 2001 Open-ended Working Group on the International Undertaking, Rome

25–30 June 2001 Sixth Extraordinary Session, Rome

22–28 April 2001 Sixth Intersessional Meeting of the Contact Group, Spoleto

5–10 February 2001 Fifth Intersessional Meeting of the Contact Group, Rome

12–17 November 2000 Fourth Intersessional Meeting of the Contact Group, Neuchâtel

26–31 August 2000 Third Intersessional Meeting of the Contact Group, Tehran

3–7 April 2000 Second Intersessional Meeting of the Contact Group, Rome

20–24 September1999 First Intersessional Meeting of the Contact Group, Rome

19–23 April 1999 Eighth Regular Session, Rome

8–12 June 1998 Fifth Extraordinary Session, Rome

1–5 December 1997 Fourth Extraordinary Session, Rome

15–23 May 1997 Seventh Regular Session, Rome

9–13 December 1996 Third Extraordinary Session, Rome

22–27 April 1996 Second Extraordinary Session, Rome

19–30 June 1995 Sixth Regular Session, Rome

7–11 November 1994 First Extraordinary Session, Rome

19–23 April 1993 Fifth Regular Session, Rome

CPGR-Ex1/94/3

Revision of the International Undertaking: Mandate, context, background and proposed process

CPGR-6/95/8 (CPGR-Ex1/94/5)

Revision of the International Undertaking: Issues for consideration in Stage II: Access to plant genetic resources, and Farmers' Rights

CPGR-6/95/8 Supp. (CPGR-Ex1/94/5 Supp.)

Revision of the International Undertaking: Analysis of some technical, economic, and legal aspects for consideration in Stage II

CPGR-6/95/9

Revision of the International Undertaking: Stage III: legal and institutional options

CGRFA-Ex3/96/LIM/2

Options for access to plant genetic resources and the equitable sharing of the benefits arising from their use

CGRFA-Ex5/98/Inf.1

Technical aspects involved in developing a list of crops for the Multilateral System within the revised International Undertaking

CGRFA-Ex5/98/Inf.1 Annex

Relevant characteristics of the crops and genera in the *Tentative List of Crops* annexed to Article 11 of the Consolidated Negotiating Text

CGRFA-8/99/8

Possible formulas for the sharing of benefits based on different benefit-indicators

CGRFA-8/99/9

Revision of the International Undertaking: Legal and Institutional Options

CGRFA-8/99/Inf.3

Exploring options for the list approach within the revised International Undertaking - Report on an informal Workshop of Experts convoked by the 'Instituto Agronomico per l'Oltremare' on behalf of the Italian Ministry of Foreign Affairs - Florence, 1-3 October 1998

C 99/9 (30th Session of the FAO Conference)

Report on progress in the revision of the International Undertaking on Plant Genetic Resources

C 99 Report (30th Session of the FAO Conference)

Draft Report on Item 8: Revision of the International Undertaking on Plant Genetic Resources

CGRFA/CG-4/00/Inf.4

Information provided by the regions on the List during the Third Inter-sessional Meeting of the Contact Group

CGRFA-9/02/17 (Ninth Regular Session)

Potential impacts of genetic use restriction technologies (GURTs) on agricultural biodiversity and agricultural production systems: technical study, Rome, 14-18 October 2002.

UNEP/CBD/SBSTTA/9/INF/6-UNEP/CBD/WG8J/3/INF/2

Report of the *ad hoc* technical expert group meeting on the potential impacts of genetic use restriction technologies on smallholder farmers, indigenous and local communities and farmers' rights, 29 September 2003.

Background Study Papers prepared during the Treaty Negotiations

Background Study Paper No.1, 1994, The appropriation of the benefits of plant genetic resources for agriculture: an economic analysis of the alternative mechanisms for biodiversity conservation (T. Swanson, D.W. Pearce and R. Cervigni, Centre for Social and Economic Research on the Global Environment, University of East Anglia).

Background Study Paper No.2, 1994, Sovereign and property rights over plant genetic resources (Carlos Correa, Professor of the Economics of Science and Technology, University of Buenos Aires).

Background Study Paper No.3, 1994, Providing Farmers' Rights through *in situ* conservation of crop genetic resources (Stephen Brush, Professor of Applied Behavioral Science, University of California, Davis).

Background Study Paper No.4, 1994, Identifying genetic resources and their origin: the capabilities and limitations of modern biochemical and legal systems (J.J. Hardon, B. Vosman and Th. J.L.van Hintum, Centre for Plant Breeding and Reproduction Research, Wagenigen, Netherlands).

Background Study Paper No.5, 1998, Information on *ex situ* collections maintained in botanic gardens (J.E. Hernandez Bermeyo, Director, Botanic Garden, Cordoba, Professor, University of Cordoba).

Background Study Paper No.6, 1997, Genetic improvements for maintaining diversity in agricultural crops (F Nuez, J.J. Ruiz and J Prohens, Polytechnic University of Valencia, Spain).

Background Study Paper No.7, 1999, Contribution to the estimation of countries' interdependence in the area of plant genetic resources (Ximena Flores Palacios, Environmental Economist, Consultant to Bolivian Ministry of Sustainable Development).

Background Study Paper No.8, 1999, Access to plant genetic resources and intellectual property rights (Carlos Correa, Professor of the Economics of Science and Technology, University of Buenos Aires).

Background Study Paper No.9, 1999, Recent developments in biotechnology as they relate to plant genetic resources for food and agriculture (Charles Spillane, Biotechnology Researcher, University College, Cork).

Background Study Paper No.10, 1999, Recent developments in biotechnology as they relate to animal genetic resources for food and agriculture (E.P. Cunningham, Professor of Animal Genetics, Trinity College, Dublin, former Director of Animal Production and Health Division, FAO).

Background Study Paper No.11, 2001, Nutritional value of some of the crops under discussion in the development of a Multilateral System (Nutrition Division, FAO).

Background Study Paper No.12, 2001, Crops proposed for the Multilateral System: centres of diversity, locations of *ex situ* collections, and major producing countries (International Plant Genetic Resources Institute).

Background Study Paper No.13, 2001, Financing treaty operations and implementation: a survey of mechanisms (Susan Bragdon, Senior Researcher, IPGRI).

Background Study Paper No.14, 2001, Transaction costs of germplasm exchange under bilateral agreements (B. Visser, Centre For Genetic Resources, Wagenigen, Netherlands, N. Louwaars, Plant Research Institute, Wagenigen, D. Eaton, Agricultural Economics Research, the Hague, J. Engels, IPGRI).

www.ingramcontent.com/pod-product-compliance
Lightning Source LLC
Chambersburg PA
CBHW041101050426
42334CB00064B/3439